How to be more positive,
enjoy life and get results.

POSITIVITY

ARTI HALAI

© Arti Halai

ISBN 978-1-906316-46-4

Published in 2009 by HotHive Books, Evesham, UK.
www.thehothive.com

The right of Arti Halai to be identified as the author of
this work has been asserted by her in accordance with the
Copyright, Designs and Patents Act 1988.

Printed in the UK by TJ International, Padstow.

To my parents,
Radha and Samji B Halai
– you are amazing.
I'm proud to be your daughter.

Arti Halai is a broadcaster, businesswoman, public speaker and author.

Her media career spans more than 15 years during which time she has worked as a TV presenter, reporter and producer for ITV1 in the Midlands, where she was known as the face of Central News. She has also worked for the BBC, ITN News Channel, Carlton, LWT, Mirror Group and Sunrise Radio.

Arti set up her first training company, AH Action (www.ahaction.com), in 2007. She is co-founder of Fleet Street Consulting Ltd (www.fleetstreetconsulting.co.uk), a consultancy devoted to helping businesses by using the power of communication.

Every year Arti is invited to present at a variety of live events and she supports a number of charities across the Midlands.

Positivity is her first book.

> ACKNOWLEDGEMENTS

My heartfelt thanks to all the people I have met on my journey.
Too many names to mention here, but you know who you are!
This book simply wouldn't have been written without you.

My sincere gratitude to the team at The HotHive, Sue
Richardson, Peter Chadwick, Katie Powell, Ceri Gautama and
especially the talent that is Sara Drinkwater and Mark Hobin.
The pleasure was all mine.

Katherine Hieronymus from Infinite Ideas – I am grateful to
you for your kindness, guidance and time.

Ken Langdon from KPL Associates – this book wouldn't be
what it is without your valuable input. I'm so delighted we met.

My beautiful sisters, Raj, Neeta, Veena and Poonam –
thanks for always being there when I need you, and my
brother-in-law, Baz, for your patience and support.

Most of all, to my husband, Zafar – the brightest star
I know – what would I do without you? Your strength,
encouragement and love continue to take me forward
and for that – you get hugs and kisses.

> CONTENTS

INTRODUCTION 9

1. FEAR 13

2. MOMENTUM 17

3. BREAKING THE ROUTINE 23

4. RECONNECT 27

5. QUALITY PEOPLE 31

6. COMPLIMENTS 35

7. TIME 41

8. A PERSONAL TOUCH 47

9. NEW OPPORTUNITIES 51

10. CHOICE 57

11. LAUGHTER 61

12. INVESTMENT 67

13. MOODS 73

14. TALENT 79

15. SAY 'NO' 83

16. ATTACHMENTS 89

17. THE PRESENT 95

18. COMPLETION 99

19. EXCELLENCE 103

20. TIME OUT 109

21. LIFESTYLE 113

22. JUST ASK 119

23. RESPONSIBILITY 123

24. SIMPLICITY 129

25. DISCIPLINE 133

26. IDENTITY 137

27. THE REALITY 143

28. PROMISES 147

29. UNDER PRESSURE 153

30. THE JOURNEY 157

'Look outside you. Think it's everything? It's nothing.

Look inside you. It is the only thing.

Master this and you master everything'

Zafar Karim, Financier

I wrote this book for me – because I had to prove to myself that I could do it; and for you – because I figured that what I had learnt was worth sharing.

We're always on the go, there is always something more to do, someone else to see – there's no denying it, our lives move at a fast pace. But what happens when you put the brakes on and stop – just for a moment?

Over the years I've had the chance to do that more than once. To look back at some of the things that I have done, achieved and experienced, both in my career and in my personal life. I've also had the chance to take a note of those things that didn't work, never materialised or were hard lessons to learn. All these things combine to make me who I am today. They've shaped my character, the results I have achieved and they continue to guide me on my journey forward. Sounds so obvious, doesn't it? But actually what I have discovered is quite profound.

How many of us actually take a moment to think about what makes us who we are? We all have a story. In the following pages you'll find bits and pieces of mine. This is part autobiography; it's bound to be since the lessons I have learnt have come from my experience and my history. Each chapter will give you an insight into my life – both on a personal and business level. They will also present the philosophies, the psychology, the lessons learnt and knowledge that I have built up over my life to date. No one concept or idea could encompass all of that, so I've used 30 of them for you to dip into and use at your leisure. Each chapter represents one day – a kind of journal – and shows you how I put my thought processes and the lessons I have learnt to good use – and how you could do the same.

It will become clear to you quite quickly that the lessons are very simple and easy to grasp; some of them are really no more than good old-fashioned common sense. But we all need a reminder or a refresher once in a while.

I'll share with you the things I learnt from my career working as a television presenter, becoming a public speaker and creating a business from scratch. I'll talk about the importance of building and nurturing relationships, giving back to others and reveal a few other secrets about myself too. While my achievements are important to me, perhaps even more crucial are the thought processes that I developed along the way. I mean, how did I become such a positive person working in a newsroom, where pretty much all news was bad news? What was it that got me from being terrified of speaking in public to teaching presentation skills to others?

I hope there will be something for everyone in this book; that among the pages you will find something to suit your needs. I've taken the liberty of providing you with some ideas and have hopefully planted these 'seeds' to help you apply what worked for me to your own situation. But just take what works for you and put it into practice.

I have deliberately made all the chapters short. I like to keep things simple and to the point, so you can use this book any way to suit you. Some people like to read in a logical manner, from start to finish. Others like to open a book on any page and take the message. Either way is fine. I like to do both, and as this book is a reflection of me I've chosen to write it in that way. Keep it by your bedside, in your top drawer, in your bag or somewhere else to hand. Dip in and out of it or read it all in one sitting – you decide.

Ultimately, like so many who have willingly given me a helping hand, I am trying to extend that to you. Take it – and use it. Then write to me and tell me all about your story – I'd love to hear it. You can reach me at www.ahaction.com or email me at arti@ahaction.com.

'Each time we face our fear, we gain strength, courage and confidence in the doing'

Anonymous

It feels as though I have spent two days looking at a blank screen on my laptop. The truth is, I don't know how to start writing a book. I have, however, committed to doing it, by deliberately telling people that I would have a book out by the end of this year; so there really is no going back.

I'm apprehensive and excited at the same time. But the emotion of *fear* is the stronger. Who am I to write a book? What if I can't find a publisher? What if the readers don't like it and I get poor reviews? Do I have enough material? And the biggest fear of all: what if it doesn't meet my expectations and the high standards I try to maintain?

I'm waiting for that touch of magic called inspiration, but as I'm doomed if it doesn't arrive, it's better to press the keys and just get started. And therein lies the first message. If you're going to eat an elephant, start with its tail.

'I'm not afraid of storms, for I'm learning how to sail my ship'

Louisa May Alcott, American Novelist

Don't run away from fear. If you do, it will only start to play on your mind and left to its own devices, unconfronted, it will grow bigger and bigger, eventually turning into a hideous, all-consuming monster. The longer you put that tricky action plan off, the more difficult it becomes – it's called putting a problem in the 'too-hard inbox'.

The key is always to tackle your fear head on, even run towards it if you have to. When you face your fear, you often realise that whatever you thought was going to happen doesn't. Somehow, nothing is ever quite as bad as you thought it was going to be.

Muster the courage and take the first steps, knowing that you have inside you, somewhere, all the strength you could ever need. You just have to give it a chance to rise to the surface. Trust yourself more. Stop thinking about it, and just get on and do it.

'Do not let what you cannot do interfere with what you can do'

John Wooden, American basketball coach

Think of your fear as a sleeping dragon – a monster – slay it, stand up to it, laugh at it, dare it to do its worst – do whatever helps you combat it. But don't let it take another moment of your time. That fear is using up too much valuable brain power and your thoughts need to be free for other, more positive and productive things.

Here's what to do with fear: confront it. Eventually you will conquer it, because circumstances dictate that you have to, the situation demands it or you realise that it prevents you from doing the things you really want to do. Tackling our fear makes us become better and stronger.

A writer friend of mine got an unusual and unexpected bad review of one of his books. He was taken aback and his self-confidence took a huge knock. What did he do? He hugged the monster by sending the review to everyone he could think of in the publishing business. The responses reminded him of his skills and how other people regarded them.

Okay, I've done it; I've written the first 500 words of the book I have promised myself, and other people of course, that I would write. That monster is maybe not dead yet, there's a long way to go, but it's under control.

'Success requires first
expending ten units of effort
to produce one unit of results.
Your momentum will then
produce ten units of results
with each unit of effort'

Charles J. Givens, US Author

> 2 MOMENTUM

Another day means at least another 500 words to write. I know the only way I will write this book is to tackle it bit by bit. Thinking of it as a whole book with 30 chapters makes it one big mammoth task too many.

So, the key is to do a tiny little amount every day. One key message, a couple of hundred words and before I know it there will be plenty of material by my six-month deadline. Thinking of my project in this way actually inspires me to put words on paper because now it feels achievable.

However, I must never lose sight of how the book will look once it is finished. I can see the cover of my book – a bright red glossy cover and the title written in large font, going across it. That's enough to keep me going.

I don't have a particular time to sit down and write, either. Why restrict yourself? Keep boundaries broad, but be clear about what you say you will achieve. I know that if I insisted on writing at a particular time of day, and then one day missed the slot then I would have an excuse to hand for not catching up later, feel disappointed and it would take much more effort to go back to the book. So, having a whole 24 hours to choose from, to dip into the project, works well for me.

'It is not of importance where we stand, but in what direction we are moving'

Anonymous

If we feel something is just too far from our reach we procrastinate and make excuses. Trust me, it doesn't matter how desperately you want that amazing thing, which of course promises to make your life perfect. If you focus on how far away the big picture of it is, you will be defeated before you even start. Chances are you will have given up long before making it to the start line.

Many people who work for large organisations for example, dream about setting up their own company, but unless they start planning and doing something about it, a dream it will remain. Why? Because it is always easier to think about the things you want, than to strive to achieve them.

Some of you may set off by approaching a project energetically and enthusiastically – at least initially, but when the quick results you expected and feel you deserved were nowhere to be seen, you discarded the project, the dream disintegrated and what did you do? Having lost momentum you moved on.

You know what I'm saying, don't you? Remember how many times you said you would get fit, eat healthier and lose those extra pounds?

A friend of mine decided to run the London Marathon for the first time. I was in awe – running 26 miles is not something that I would ever even contemplate doing. But each to their own, and he showed real commitment to the task. He trained hard for it – at first running a few miles a week then building up the stamina to do 15 miles and more at a time.

On the day he did well. Afterwards, I asked him what kept him going during the toughest part of the race, which he suffered at around the 22-mile mark. He told me he picked a point further up the track, and kept saying to himself, 'If I can make it to that point, then I know I will be fine'.

'If you can imagine it you can achieve it, if you can dream it you can become it'

William Arthur Ward, American author

Take a look at something that you started, but failed to complete. Think about what got you started in the first place. Create a Polaroid picture in your mind of what it will be like when the project is finished.

Then, don't beat yourself up about not achieving it but commit to doing something small and manageable to get back on track. Agree to do it every day, once a week, or in whatever timescale is right for you.

Simply achieving this first thing will make you feel good and encourage you to keep going.

··· TRY THIS ···

Then an amazing thing will happen – you will have created one of the keys to achieving your outcome – momentum.

Climbers always say when climbing the mountain not to look up towards the summit. All you will see is an endless stretch of brightness in front of you, and all you will feel are the harsh realities of the bitter cold. Focus instead on the steps you are taking one at a time – and before you know it, you will have reached the top!

The Taj Mahal was not built in a day. Consistently working at something with purpose produces far greater rewards and satisfaction than you can ever imagine.

I know I'm only at the start of my project, but so far so good. I've completed two chapters now and actually the cogs are already turning about what I might do tomorrow.

'It is easier to find an excuse than to find a reason'

Doug Brown, author

> 3 BREAKING THE ROUTINE

I know I've been naughty. I have neglected to write the minimum 500 words I promised myself that I would do to get this book off the ground for at least five days now. At first, I felt guilty. I even made an effort to write something one day, but the words just wouldn't come out right. So then I 'took the rest of the week off' – well, almost. After a week of feeling fired up and writing my promised 500 words daily, I broke the routine. But it wasn't my fault – honest!

I went on a business trip and had to spend a few days in another city. Did I mention that I have a training company? AH Action specialises in presentation skills, media training and communication skills. Part of my research involves looking at new psychological and personal development strategies. Hence the meeting with a person who also happens to be my friend – don't you just love it when things work out like that?

She wanted to share some new material on personality profiling with me, and I wanted to discuss a course that I was putting together for a group of lawyers with her. I had three days for the sessions pencilled in my diary.

I was concerned about breaking both my routine and the momentum I had built up. I had no intention of failing to achieve what I had set out to do but the interruption had the potential to throw a spanner in the works. That three-day meeting had been planned for months, and I knew that if I postponed, it would be another two months before I could reschedule. Not an option. So I went to the meetings and broke the routine.

On my return, I knew it had been the right thing to do. The meetings had been excellent and I came back with fresh insight and useful knowledge. But now I felt guilty and getting back to the book was becoming a real struggle. Then it dawned on me that I was using the break in my routine as an excuse. Somewhere along the way I had decided that everything would just go according to plan. But life isn't like that, is it?

'Where the heart is willing it will find a thousand ways, but where it is unwilling is will find a thousand excuses'

Dayak proverb

Bring to the front of your mind a routine that you had going for a project that was making good progress. Sorting out the filing system perhaps, or practising a musical instrument regularly. Whatever it is, are you beating yourself up about it? How is that making you feel right now? Is it any wonder you haven't resumed the routine? Stop feeling guilty, think about the break as a part of everyday life, and get back to doing something towards it. ··· TRY THIS ···

Take the action. It is never too late. Sometimes we have to do things slightly differently to get to our final destination.

Back to my work schedule: I've just had one meeting and am waiting for another one, but today for the first time I packed my laptop, thinking I could put it to good use as I sit in a coffee shop killing a little time. And hey presto, what do you know? I'm making the most of my lost time. The amazing thing is that when I buckle down to the writing I actually really enjoy the process. However I can sometimes spend so much time thinking about how I haven't done what I promised myself that I start to dread getting back into the flow.

A change of scene can help too. Sitting here in a coffee shop, absorbing the sounds around me, seeing people engaged in conversation, watching others come and go – this all helps me get back into the swing of things.

I know someone who constantly comes up with lots of business ideas. He does the research for some of them but before long he has moved on to the next big thing. He hardly ever sees anything through to completion. As a result he has very little to show for his work.

Another colleague of mine was always on a diet, until she realised it is ok to go off course, as long as you don't lose sight of the track and that big picture of the final achievement. When at first she would lapse and taste the forbidden food she always felt so guilty, and worse, thought that others were judging her. She would then ditch the plan altogether. Now she understands that being rigid and strict about the way things should be done is not the answer.

So pick up something you know you need to complete and get on with it. Life really is too short.

'It's not too late to develop friendships or reconnect with people'

Morrie Schwartz, US educator and author

Whoever said life would be easy? I don't understand why so many people want to write a book! It's a really hard challenge to fit it in with the rest of your busy life. I've been a journalist for 15 years and, hand on heart, I'm still not sure I am cut out for the job – and by that I mean writing this book. Still, as promised I am putting pen to paper and sharing my next idea.

Today I have pottered around my loft in Birmingham and spent the morning reading a book called *How to Have a Beautiful Mind* by Edward de Bono, a leading authority in the field of creative thinking. I've spent the bulk of my time doing two things: one for myself, and the other something I promised myself I would do this year. The former is not so important: I lost myself in the book, eating potato waffles, after reminding myself that I have a gym session at 8am tomorrow morning. The latter involved making time for people I know are an integral part in my life, but for whatever reason, perhaps I take for granted.

'Humankind has not woven the web of life. We are but one thread within it. Whatever we do to the web, we do to ourselves. All things are bound together. All things connect'

Chief Seattle, leader of the Suquamish and Duwamish Native American tribes

This year I made a conscious decision to make more of an effort with those I need to reconnect with. These include my cousins abroad and my sisters – all four of them. I maintain contact with two of them at least once a week, but my oldest and youngest sisters I need to work on actively – I know I have to do this, since over the years I've felt that we've been drifting apart.

If the captain of a ship is one degree off course every day then the distance between where the ship is and where it should be over time becomes vast.

As usual, I pressed speed dial and called my middle two sisters. I had a great conversation with both. Before I put the phone down, I was subtly reminded to call my youngest sister, as I had promised I would do. The reality is that I had actually forgotten. Guilt surged through me.

I dialled my youngest sister's number. What transpired was a wonderful 50-minute conversation. We talked about all sorts of things, and she lifted my spirits. She made me feel important; I wonder if she knew that.

How did she do this? She never made me feel guilty or questioned my motives for the call. She simply seemed pleased to hear my voice, and didn't make the conversation difficult. As our chat progressed, she asked advice about certain situations that I had already gone through in life. She was genuinely interested in my life and how I was dealing with my struggles. And what's more, she started to open up to me, and to share things she had experienced, albeit in a rather careful and guarded way.

Who have you drifted away from? How much do they mean to you? What is stopping you from reconnecting with them again? Don't dwell on what you think their response will be, or why they haven't got in touch with you. Stop asking questions and start dialling, writing, e-mailing or going to see them. It is never too late to reconnect with someone.

An ex-colleague of mine was suddenly widowed. She was in shock and grief for a long time. Then one day she told a friend of hers that one of the things she really missed was having someone to go to classical concerts with. It was something her husband and she had done frequently. Her friend reminded her of a man they had gone to university with. He used to enjoy going to concerts too but over time they had all got too busy doing their own thing and failed to keep in touch. The distance between them had grown over the years. Still, she reconnected with him through a mutual friend. Now they escort each other to concerts on a regular basis.

'From now on, I'll connect the dots my own way'

Bill Watterson, American author

Some people touch our lives, make us feel special; we miss them and want to reignite the feelings we get from being with them. So what are you waiting for? Go and reconnect with someone. You know it's the right thing to do.

'A single conversation with a wise man is better than ten years of study'

Chinese proverb

> 5 QUALITY PEOPLE

I made a conscious decision last year to meet at least two new people every month – and no cheating. They had to be what *I* call 'quality' people.

So what is my definition of a quality person? This is somebody who, within minutes of conversation, I recognise and admire as an achiever. From entrepreneurs and senior management to those working on the shop floor or in a back room, regardless of sector or industry, voluntary or paid. For me a quality person transcends all barriers, races and classes.

A quality person doesn't need to sell what they do, but leads you to buy into them. Conversation flows easily and smoothly over a number of topics, and energy is transferred effortlessly. Time just flies and you enjoy every second of the meeting. They give generously without demanding anything back – quite a tall order then!

Over the years I have been fortunate to meet a wide range of quality people. In business, a few people in particular come to mind. They are all big players in the business world, with very different personalities engaged in very different things. They're really busy too.

I've learnt a variety of things from them. One taught me about the need for clarity and drive, another immediately included me in his inner circle and opened doors for me and the third helped me to raise the bar and introduced me to the reality of ambition. Strange really, that this is the first time that I have actually thought about how specifically they have helped me on my business journey. When we meet up it is always so much fun. . . and the last thing we seem to talk about is work.

The other thing about quality people is that you never know when or where you will meet them. I was delighted when on my way to a business meeting one morning, I bumped into one of the 'quality' contacts I mentioned before. I hadn't seen him in a while. We exchanged pleasantries, touched base briefly about what was going on, and before departing we pencilled a lunch in the diary. Not bad for an unexpected ten-minute chance encounter! I smiled all the way to my next appointment. Quality people have the ability to make you do that.

'You can easily judge the character of a man by how he treats those who can do nothing for him'

James D Miles

Quality people are those from whom you can learn. They assist you to grow and develop and make you feel good about yourself. They make time for you. But it is not all about business. Quality people exist everywhere. You just have to recognise them.

·· TRY THIS ··

Make a list of people that you know whom you would class as 'quality' people. Think back to the different stages in your life, and people who have guided you or taken you under their wing. What is it that makes them so special? What have you specifically learnt from them? How much of that have you put into practice? Has some of that useful mentoring worn off?

·· TRY THIS ··

Another type of quality person is somebody whose path crossed yours at a certain moment in time. It may be somebody from the past who you've lost touch with but will always remember.

For example, a few years ago I was invited to a school to talk to a group of 11-year-olds who were not doing well in the education system. As a TV presenter, I was asked to give the youngsters my story about how I got into the media industry. So I told them about the trials and tribulations of being a presenter. They gasped when I told them I got up at 4 o'clock in the morning to do the breakfast shift, and laughed when I told them about bad hair days.

Then they told me about their project. Their teacher had involved them in a scheme where they were each asked to mentor and assist a three-year-old child from a nearby nursery. They spoke excitedly and with pride about their protégés, the pictures they helped them paint and the games they played. Crucially, being tasked with such a responsibility raised their confidence, self-esteem and expectations. For me that teacher is, and always will be, a 'quality' person.

I know you too are a quality person for someone, somewhere. Making the time for somebody else really is a wonderful feeling. After all, what goes around, comes around – in abundance.

'When you cannot get a compliment any other way, pay yourself one'

Mark Twain, US novelist and humorist

> 6 COMPLIMENTS

Why do people always get embarrassed when they are paid a compliment?

'Oh, you look great!' meets with, 'You're just saying that!'
'I like what you're wearing' is met with, 'Oh, it's just a cheap little number'.

Stop it, now! Never do it again! When somebody pays you a compliment, just accept it. It should be the best feeling in the world. I learnt this a long time ago, especially as a TV presenter in the public eye. Presenting the bulletins regularly for a number of years in the Midlands meant people recognised me. Viewers would often come up and say hello and how much they enjoyed watching me in the mornings. At first I used to get embarrassed, but I soon realised it was part and parcel of the job and once I got over that I accepted their gracious remarks and thanked them for coming to talk to me.

Receiving compliments has made me more positive, more confident and it means that people like to be around me. Blowing my own trumpet? So what? That's what I am told, and I choose to accept it, believe it. It's like a cycle, if you accept compliments and believe them you will become them, meriting them even more.

This is not about being arrogant. Here's the difference. Somebody arrogant comes across as inflated, self-absorbed and not interested in conversation unless it involves and revolves around them. They also have a tendency to 'big themselves up' with the intention of putting the other person down.

Compliments help to build somebody up and can inspire them to do even better. Compliments give you a smile that can light up your eyes. Compliments make you feel taller and stronger. Think about it for a moment – when somebody tells you something good about yourself, how does it make you feel?

I was at an event last night and one of the guests said to me, 'I'm telling this young woman what a good job she does at work, but she doesn't believe me. What would you say to her to give her more confidence?' It was obvious that the young woman and the man, who was a senior manager, had been talking for a while. I turned to the young woman and explained to her that her boss was telling her what he thought about her work. He must have seen the quality of what she did and appreciated her input.

His compliment was genuine and seemed to come from an earlier conversation they were having. I told her to accept what he had said gracefully and thank him for it. I left her with a little something to think about. 'Why would you want to constantly put yourself down or think that you are not good enough?'

When you start to feel good about yourself, then your confidence grows. Accept compliments at face value and reflect only on negative criticism to check whether it is right or not.

'What flatterers say, try to make true'

German proverb

I remember one evening, with time to spare, I was wondering around a shopping mall before moving on to a dinner party. As I was coming down the escalator I spotted a woman on the other side going up. I didn't think anything of it. Then as I started walking towards the exit, I heard someone running up behind me. The woman stopped me and politely said, 'I just wanted you to know that you look lovely in that outfit'.

I was blown away. Touched that a total stranger was willing to take the effort to come back down the escalator and make my day. I thanked her, and went on my way, with a big smile and a spring in my step.

Accepting a compliment is one side of the coin – paying a compliment is the other. It's not hard. When you see something that you like, go and tell that person. It could be anybody. Don't restrict yourself to just your spouse, partner, friends, relatives or work colleagues. Why not the supermarket attendant, taxi driver or someone you end up in a lift with? How often do we tell someone cleaning a loo in a restaurant that they're doing a good job? Try it and watch the response.

Make a conscious effort to pay at least two people a genuine compliment today. Note how they respond. Also take into account how it made you feel.

Think about the last time someone paid you a compliment. How did you react? What will you do next time? When did you last give a big thank you to someone who is important to you?

Phone your daughter or son, or someone else close to you and tell them how proud you are of them.

A friend of mine is an actor. He told me that the best part of the night for him is standing on stage after a performance to thunderous applause. He sees it as the audience's way of paying him a compliment and he revels in the moment. So he should. You will never see an actor rush off stage or look shy and timid after a show. They take their time and appreciate the moment fully. It is a mutually gratifying experience for both the entertainer and the entertained.

Remember, when you make a conscious effort to praise someone, it comes back tenfold. Not only have you made someone's day, but you'll feel good about it too.

Of course, there is no point in doing anything if you don't really mean it. Compliments only work when they are genuinely given and received.

'But what minutes! Count them by sensation, and not by calendars, and each moment is a day'

Benjamin Disraeli, British politician

> 7 TIME

Alas, time is the one thing we all have the same amount of, and never get back. Twenty-four precious hours, spread over a day and a night.

Are you using yours productively? Not always, is the confession I choose to make today. In fact, of late, my timing has been out of synch. My sleep pattern has taken on a life of its own. I find myself waking up at 3 o'clock in the morning and staying that way till 5.30am, tossing and turning in bed. What this means is that when the alarm goes off, whereas once I used to jump out of bed with a spring in my step, I now struggle, blinking manically and thinking every morning is still the middle of the night. Why am I writing business proposals at 10.30 at night? Surely that is the sort of work I should be doing during the day? Since when did breakfast start at midday?

Everybody has their own theory on time; how to use it, manage it, get more of it and how not to waste it. I believe that, just as we change, grow and develop, so does our timing in life. Let me explain. When you are a child, bedtime is often early at around 7.30 or 8 o'clock at night. However, as you get older this changes and you stay up longer and get to bed much later. When was the last time you went to bed at around 8 o'clock? That is what I mean about your timing in life changing.

I know this sounds a little weird, but just hear me out. Things happen. Our circumstances change, as do our surroundings, along with our thought patterns and our lifestyles. Our timing is connected to it all.

'It is how we spend our time here and now, that really matters. If you are fed up with the way you have come to interact with time, change it'

Marcia Wieder, American author and speaker

I know some writers who get up early and are tapping away at their novels at 5 o'clock in the morning, before rushing out to do the day job. They are alert and enjoy the serenity the dawn brings with it, as the rest of the world lies soundly asleep. I'm not one of them. . . at least not anymore. . . or more accurately, not at the moment.

Actually, when I used to present the breakfast bulletins, I needed to be bright-eyed and ready for action in the newsroom by 5am. Getting up and to work on time was never a problem. In fact I enjoyed it. But now that it is no longer part of the daily requirement, I'm struggling. The most amazing thing about that shift was how much I actually managed to accomplish in such a short period of time.

Reading the bulletins was one thing, but I was also producing them. I did everything by the clock – each task like trawling through the news agency wires, chasing stories, researching and rewriting material, calling police and fire stations. I had to do everything by a certain time. I could not miss anything out, and there was plenty to do. It was an extremely productive and effective use of my time and effort.

There is no wrong or right time to do things – just make it work for you. Of course you need to be practical and realistic, but if you find yourself alert and more productive at certain times of the day, then choose those moments to do what needs to be done. If your body clock has taken on a life of its own, then so be it. Eventually your timing will settle into a suitable pattern again. But is there any point in fighting something you don't really understand?

Better to tap into your most resourceful time and achieve what you need to. After all, we have to meet our deadlines, we need to spend time with our loved ones, we need to manage our businesses. Trust me, if you think about it and plan the use of your time it will all get done. There should even be time left over for you to indulge in, if you use it well.

'The bad news is time flies. The good news is you're the pilot'

Michael Altshuler, Motivational speaker

When you focus on something and channel your energy in the right way, you get more done – results in faster time. Just don't try to do everything. Choose what you are going to do, reject other activities and plan how you will achieve it all. The key message here is to use less time to achieve more.

Do you feel the pressure of the looming deadline? Are you suffering guilt pangs after taking a stroll in the park instead of working? Have you been surfing the web or catching up with a friend on the phone, when you shouldn't have been? Think of that as time well spent, because you can now buckle down to the task at hand.

Notice how long it takes you to do – did it take as long as you thought it would or did you complete the task much faster?

Notice at what times of the day you tend to be most productive. Try to do the most important task in that period. If you don't have anything pressing then look down your list of things to do, find the most unattractive thing and do that first.

··· TRY THIS ···

The job always gets done, better and quicker than it otherwise would have, when you tap into your body clock and use your time effectively.

The speed at which this book is being written is exactly down to this. I write when I most feel like it. . . and so the chapters come together quite quickly. Of course, the impending deadline helps as well.

'There are two ways of spreading light – to be the candle or the mirror that reflects it'

Edith Wharton, US novelist

Let's face it, we are born with nothing and we will leave with nothing. So why not use the time in between to create some special moments for yourself and others? I find that the small things in life make a huge difference.

The beauty in this is that these special moments don't cost a lot, if anything at all, and are readily available. They are quite simply the little things we do to show someone we appreciate them or care about them.

Think about it – how do you feel when someone gives you a present? And how do you feel when you give someone a present? Remember what it was like the last time you gave someone a present. We all revel in the excitement and anticipation showing on their face, their smile and sense of curiosity as they are just about to unwrap the gift. Either way it is a great feeling isn't it?

Of course, I'm not saying everybody will remember what you did for them or gave them – but that isn't the point. It's about how you felt at the time, what you did to improve or make someone's day.

A few months ago I was discussing an author with a friend of mine. We both enjoy reading and we were sharing our latest discoveries. Two weeks later I received a jiffy bag in the post. I felt excited – especially as I wasn't expecting anything. What I found inside was a book by the writer my friend and I had spoken about. I couldn't stop smiling: it was such a thoughtful gesture, and I was very touched.

I made a decision to do that for someone else so that they too could start their day with a smile. I posted a card with a handwritten message to a friend I hadn't spoken to for months. The card had a funny picture on the front; actually it reminded me of her and the message was both personal and heartfelt. It worked a treat, and she has kept the card to this day. I also know that it made her smile when she received it that morning.

Just like that, I helped to start someone's day in a better way, and it feels like such a small thing to do. And while I am all for immediacy and efficiency (e-mail works great most of the time), I also know the feeling of going to my letter box to check if I have received any post. Forget the standard, official-looking envelopes and the junk mail, which goes straight in the bin. I'm curious – does anybody ever read that? I'm talking about seeing real envelopes – regardless of shape, size or weight, the ones that feel like a card or things that arrive in jiffy bags! Admit it – it gets the adrenalin going.

:: TRY THIS ::

Every once in a while, surprise someone and send them something in the post. You might want to do this once a month or every season. It may be to the same person, or to different people. It could be a handwritten letter, picture, card, photograph, vouchers, a small present or anything else that you see fit. And make sure you tell them, directly or indirectly, the reason for sending the special present. For example… 'I saw this and thought of. . .', 'Something to make you smile. . .', 'Missing you. . .'.

:: TRY THIS ::

When you make an effort for someone, no matter how small, you make them feel important and let them know you care for them. There are other ways of doing small things to show someone you care for them, too; you know what they are.

A friend of mine works in the Human Resources department in a large public sector organisation. She said that an independent survey recently carried out in the department revealed that the number one complaint where she worked was that people didn't even say 'hello' to each other. How long does that take? In a department like that even offering to make a cup of tea for someone would go a long way. But we get so caught up with millions of other things that we don't do the things that really matter nearly often enough.

It is the small things that are the most important, and often mean so much to someone. They require so little in terms of resources, and yet they can create such an impact. It is these gestures that make such a huge difference to someone's day – and yours! Remember when you are open and willing to make someone else's day, someone else is open and willing to make yours.

'Too often we underestimate the power of a touch, a smile, a kind word, a listening ear, an honest compliment, or the smallest act of caring, all of which have the potential to turn a life around'

Leo F Buscaglia, American author and teacher

‘If opportunity doesn’t
knock, build a door’

Milton Berle, US comedian and actor

> 9 NEW OPPORTUNITIES

I'm having a relatively quiet week on the business front, but I'm not worried. The last two months have been remarkable – lots of work, progress on my book, and I've made contact with new people in areas where I want to grow my business and do more personal voluntary work.

But things don't just happen. I became extremely focused about both what I wanted and needed to do to get where I want to this year. It was full steam ahead, but now the pressure has eased a little, and though my diary was never overloaded, I do see more spaces in it. However I know those empty holes will start to fill up, somehow, when the moment is right.

'Change the way you look at things and the things you look at will change'

Dr Wayne Dyer

Imagine coming home after a long, hard day at work to a warm, comfortable, cosy place. The problem is you've only got about 40 minutes before you need to be on your way out again. It may be a work event, a club you've joined, a charity fundraising quiz, or a social night out with friends. It seemed like such a good idea at the time, but right now you just can't muster up the enthusiasm or energy for it.

I confess this happens to me – quite often. Eight times out of ten I have to force myself to go to work events, especially if I'm already winding down at home. A quick phone call to my amazing friend, who never fails to remind me about the importance of the commitment, in his usual charming manner – and I'm ready to act.

If truth be told, once the dress is on and the look is right, then Cinderella is raring to go. Afterwards I always have a great time. Sometimes it's the venue and ambience, sometimes the food and drink, at other times the sheer entertainment – but above all, it is the people I meet at these events that make them so memorable. I've always got to know at least one person better as a result of making the effort.

Once I spent about 15 minutes talking to someone at a charity event. Our conversation was brief but enjoyable. We exchanged a few e-mails. I didn't know at the time that he knew the director of an academic organisation who I had been trying to meet for the best part of a year. Within days of a nudge from my new friend, the door had opened and space had been made in both mine and the director's diaries for a meeting.

It always pays to make time for people.

I also like meeting lots of people from different sectors, industries, backgrounds, cultures and countries. Building new relationships is like building anything. You need to work at it. This isn't just about meeting lots of people; this is about making the effort with just one person.

Good relationships are built on mutual respect and a shared understanding.

I have discovered new opportunities and grown my business because of the network of people I have met and the relationships I have built over time. I've become a richer person, in every respect, because these people have come into my life and with them have come huge opportunities – to develop my thinking, challenge my views, experience new things and explore new places.

There is always someone you can learn more from, who can open your eyes to reveal a hidden gem, who can give you an insight into something deeper.

I've always known opportunities and people go hand in hand. And while it might work for business, it also works for any other area of your life you might want it to. This is a two-way process and while someone may be creating an opportunity for you, you could be doing the same for someone else.

A friend of mine was approaching retirement with some trepidation: he was worried about how he would pass his time. I gave him a challenge that someone had given me on a course: 'Write about what the best six months after retirement would be like for you'. He wrote about watching cricket and playing golf, his two lifetime passions. He spoke about meeting his children for lunch and so on.

When he had finished I noticed that everything he was expecting to do was already part of his life – there was nothing new there at all. He was not exploiting the new opportunity that being retired offered him.

We discussed his response and I asked him to do the exercise again, this time searching deeper and giving more detail in his answers. He is now retired and enjoying life. He goes round car boot sales and other places buying up cricket and golf memorabilia and selling them on eBay, something he learnt more about from his son's friend. He is also taking an evening class in drawing. It had never been on his radar, but he felt he wanted to try his hand at something new and different.

'Man's mind stretched to a new idea never goes back to its original dimensions'

Oliver Wendall Holmes, American physician and author

Make a point of getting to know at least one new person a month. It could be somebody at work who you only know via e-mail or on the phone. Next time you need to talk to them, make the effort to go and see them face-to-face instead. Or, if you are at a social event, go and break the ice with someone you don't know. Take the lead and see what happens.

··· TRY THIS ···

So now you know why I'm not worried about the blank spaces in my calendar. Someone new is bound to turn up and claim their rightful space in the diary – they always do.

'Guido the plumber and Michelangelo obtained their marble from the same quarry, but what each of them saw in the marble made the difference between a nobleman's sink and a sculpture'

Bob Kall, author

Horrible things can and do happen to us. It's part of life. We can't stop things happening to us, but we can choose how we are going to deal with them when they do.

Last year I was made redundant from my role as a TV presenter for a well-known company. It was such a shock; I lost a job I was both good at and enjoyed doing. I never saw it coming. I also never lost sight of the fact that the decision had been a business one; I was nothing more than a casualty of cutbacks at the company. This had nothing to do with my ability, personality, hard work or experience. I chose to look at the decision in exactly that light.

> ## 'It's choice - not chance - that determines your destiny'
>
> Jean Nidetch, author

I spent a few weeks dwelling on what had happened, what I was going to do next and the lessons I had learnt from the experience. I went through the emotions and felt sorry for myself, at least for a little while. What really helped me through it was turning to my friends and family. Over the years I have spent time building good relationships, so when I needed it most, those close to me reminded me of my good qualities, and never let my confidence dip too low.

I made a conscious decision to turn to those who knew me and had time for me. I openly spoke to them about my situation, and in return I received perspective and strength. Going back to a previous chapter, I hugged the monster. Everybody deals with things in their own way – this was my way of dealing with the nightmare.

Suffice to say, Christmas was quiet. Then with the New Year I snapped back to form. I refused to spend any more time dwelling on the past. Instead, I explored ways to grow my business, deciding to take the opportunity to do some work abroad, and write this book. I spoke to people about my plans to keep me focused about the way ahead.

'It is our choices that show what we truly are, far more than our abilities'

JK Rowling, British novelist

Telling people that I had been made redundant was especially difficult. The word 'redundant' has such negative connotations that at first, I felt embarrassed and ashamed to say it out loud. I also had to endure viewers asking, 'Why don't we see you on the box anymore?' I didn't blame them; they didn't know. How could they?

Saying that I had been made redundant was a huge personal obstacle for me to overcome. What helped was that I said it right from the start, and didn't choose to use another excuse. I'm proud of myself for making that choice and seeing it through. It was difficult at first, but (like most things) the more you do it, the more you get used to saying it. Time is, indeed, a great healer.

Think about something difficult that you are currently going through. Take a piece of paper and on one side write down what the problem is, who is involved and how it is making you feel. On the other side write down what the ideal situation would be. Take a look at how each side makes you feel. We all have choices in life; make yours work for you. When you have made your choice, write down the attitude you need to have to make the ideal come about and put it somewhere you can see it every day.

... TRY THIS ...

Years ago when I was growing up, we had a neighbour we got on well with. He used to be a heavyweight professional boxer. He'd retired and was setting up his own construction company. One day when I returned home from university, my parents told me that he had lung cancer. The disease had rapidly spread throughout his body. I went to see him. He was a shadow of his former self. His voice was a raspy whisper. But he refused to give up. His wit was sharp and instead of dwelling on the current situation he chose to talk about the good times in his life, the stars he had met, the things he had seen, the places he had visited and what he had achieved.

It doesn't matter whether it is the past or the future. What matters is what you choose to focus on. As for me I don't want to live in the past, I choose instead to focus on the present and all the new adventures I have yet to experience. I believe it is a much better place to be.

'A smile is a curve that sets everything straight'

Phyllis Diller, US actor and stand-up comedian

I'm smiling as I write this. For me, laughter is the best free medicine in the world. Remember the last time you laughed so much your belly or jaws hurt; when your eyes watered (for the right reasons); when the tears of laughter rolled down your cheeks; when you forgot about everything else for that one moment?

That uncontrollable explosion may take just one glance or a sound and, bang – you can't stop laughing. It is a great feeling. I wish I could bottle it up and sell it. Imagine a tonic that you just need to smell or taste to set you off. Wow! We would always be able to see the funny side of things. Could any day really be a bad day?

'At the height of laughter, the universe is flung into a kaleidoscope of new possibilities'

Dr Jean Houston, US author and scholar

The thing about uncontrollable laughter is that it often only takes a small thing to get you going. That sort of intense laughter is often shared between two people and you can never recapture it. Afterwards, when you look back at what started it all off, it can take a while to remember whether the trigger really was that funny in the first place. That's the thing about laughter. You can't really explain it with logic; it is uncontrollable and you never know when it will strike.

Maybe it goes back to my childhood (don't most things?). I remember as a child seeing my rather rotund aunt slip and fall on some snow, as she came out of her house. It was early morning and she was in a black and white sari. She was known for her brisk manner and coarse language (something I find entertaining to this day), and as she tried to get up, she slipped on her sari straight back down again. This went on for a while, the air turning blue with her language. You had to be there to see it; I was there and it still makes me smile when I think about it.

Now why would that be funny? It is inexplicable, and I know, inexcusable. That is the thing with laughter – it has no boundaries. You'll also find that when you try to explain what's funny to others, they won't get it. It's never that funny when you come out of the 'zone'. Take a moment and remember the last time you had a really good laugh.

More often than not, I experience the mad sort of laughter I'm talking about with my sisters. And in that way I'm fortunate, as I have four of them. Strangely, it only takes the smallest thing to set any two of us off, and most of the time nobody else seems to get the joke. This is because it is not always about a joke. It is more likely to be something that we have distorted and then tied together with a shared experience from our past.

For example, when I was young we played a game where we dipped the soles of our shoes in the fish pond at the local park and made footprints on the tiles around. Then one day I slipped and fell into the pond. We knew it meant trouble. My sister tried to secretly smuggle me into the house but it didn't work and we got caught. It wasn't funny at the time. But somehow it makes us laugh now.

Or we crack up when we think about the mad panic that ensued years ago when our car got sandwiched so tightly between two others and we realised we weren't going anywhere fast. Remembering everyone's faces, language and actions is enough to set us off. Strange, none of this seems funny on my own, but when two distorted views come together it can be rather explosive.

> ## 'A smile is an inexpensive way to change your looks'
>
> Charles Gordy, author

The best thing about laughter is the warm feeling you get when you think back to your last large outburst – I guarantee it will make you smile. I know this because the two are linked. Laughter is an extension of smiling. You can't have the one without the other. Laughter is extreme and unpredictable; smiling is contagious and can be given openly and freely. It is a language that is understood by all across the world. We do it naturally – but just in varying degrees.

Go to the mirror. Smile at yourself and see what it does to your facial features. Now look at your face as it normally is and notice how your facial expressions look. Compare the two different looks and write down what you find. How does each different facial expression make you feel? Which one do you prefer?

Every morning when you get up, smile to yourself, and every evening before you fall asleep, smile to yourself. It will make you think about the good things in your life.

Make sure that at some point today you go and smile at someone you don't know – and then see what happens.

A doctor working in a hospital in a developing country once said to me that all other matters aside, the most uplifting part of his day and what made it all worthwhile for him was seeing his patients smile. It warms the heart. It will change the way you look and feel in an instant. I'm still smiling as I come to the end of this chapter – I hope you are too.

'It's what you learn after you know it all that counts'

Attributed to **Harry S Truman**, 33rd US president

> 12 INVESTMENT

What is the best investment you can make? Property? Business? Stocks and shares? IT? Telecommunications? The list could go on. Not in my book! I think the best investment you will ever make has to be in yourself: educating yourself, expanding your knowledge and experiencing things.

Business is a little quiet at the moment so I have made the decision that it is the perfect time to go on a few training courses. Some are personal development ones, while others are business related. Some have been free and others I have paid for. Incidentally, you will be amazed at how many free courses you'll come across if you do some searches on the Internet. But the truth is that at the end of the day everything costs. Let's face it, if you aren't paying in pounds, then you are paying in time.

I used to associate education with learning and school. I was never an academic child; I always just scraped through everything. School was not a happy experience for me. However, back in 1997 I'd taken a break from the media industry and started looking for something to fill my time and keep me mentally active. I enrolled on a stress management course. It was something that excited me; something I wanted to learn more about, and most importantly something I wanted to do – successfully manage stress.

Admittedly, it was far more theoretical than I had expected. I fussed and fretted over my essays – only feeling relief after handing them in just in time. My previous school experience had not been too promising, so my expectation was low to say the least. Imagine my surprise when I scored in the 90s. It spurred me on, and I eventually passed with a distinction.

You are guaranteed better results when you want to do something yourself rather than being forced to do it. Why? Because you will put more effort in if you make the choice. My course had me delving deep into identifying the symptoms of stress and the root cause of it. I could have built on it further and gone down the counselling route, but I chose not to. My stopgap was coming to an end, and the lure back to my career in the media was too strong. It was never my intention to qualify as a counsellor; so my investment had returned what I wanted. What I got from the first part of the course was enough for me, at that moment in time.

Doing any course and getting through it is only a part of the experience – applying the knowledge is what lies at the heart of any teaching. What I soon found was that the course was becoming a real talking point. People were fascinated about what I had learnt, and by sharing my insights with them, I could keep the teachings alive. I'm sure there are still aspects of it I use today, along with all the new knowledge I have picked up over time.

'There are some things you learn best in calm, and some in storm'

Willa Cather, American author

Growing and developing doesn't always have to be about qualifying in something, getting points or ticking the boxes. It doesn't have to be about just doing something in one particular way. Everything is constantly growing, evolving and changing. The only constant in life is change.

My mum first came to the UK as a young, naive woman in the late 1960s, having married my dad. She wholeheartedly embraced her role as a housewife and brought up five girls in a loving home. She was strict but instilled in us a regard for tradition and culture and the need to respect others.

Now that her girls have all grown up and are doing their own things, my mum has seized the opportunity to invest in learning new things for herself. She decided that she wanted to learn more about computers, so she went and enrolled on an evening class. She openly admitted she struggled with it, but she stuck at it and now we're all able to exchange e-mails with her. For her, sharing e-mails with her children is a terrific return on her investment. And she's not stopping there either. She's moving on from the beginners' course to the advanced level. It is never too late to learn.

What I've learnt over the years is simple. We're always learning, whether it is out of need or choice. It can be a struggle but it can also be lots of fun. Learning keeps us young and alive.

When I am running training courses myself, the first thing I say to my clients is 'just take the information that works for you'. Do any training with an open mind. Then take what you have learnt, and combine it with your previous knowledge to create something new and special that works for you.

··· TRY THIS ···

When was the last time you learnt something new for yourself? Remember, going on a training course isn't the only way to learn. Spend some time with somebody who has a special skill and observe them. Find somebody who is willing to tell you what they have learnt through their experiences. Listen to a CD, watch something on the box or surf the net. Ask yourself 'What have I learnt today?'

··· TRY THIS ···

I know of a woman who changed her life after asking herself what she had learnt that day. Her answer was basically nothing since she was bringing up two children and working as a child minder. It made her think about doing something to stretch herself beyond her obvious expertise in looking after children. Not much later, she enrolled in the Open University, taking four years to get a good degree by studying only in the evenings. She then did a social work course and when her children were old enough, became a social worker. What a waste of her talent it would have been, had she not asked herself the question 'What did I learn today?' and then worked like stink to learn and develop.

There is no wrong way or right way when it comes to investing in yourself – just do it your way. We are all lifelong learners.

'I don't wait for moods.
You accomplish nothing
if you do that. Your mind
must know it has got to get
down to work'

Pearl S Buck, US writer

Today is going to be a bad day and it serves me right! For starters, I ignored my alarm, stayed in bed too long, and then woke up angry with myself. I missed doing my exercise video, and then cleverly justified it by telling myself that I was aching from a hard gym session the day before.

Then the nightmare – I had to pack for a three-day course in London. How does one pack for these sorts of things? I'm great if I need to pack for a hot holiday, but a few days in another city in the UK – now that's difficult!

I had a business meeting to attend before the journey too. I needed to have enough smart wear for the three-day course and some casual stuff for the evenings. I also had a fundraising ball to go to on the Friday night – so dress, sandals, evening handbag and coat all had to find space in my little bag. It was a real trauma.

I don't like packing or unpacking at the best of times – but it goes hand in hand with travelling, which I simply adore. Looking back I think it was the packing that played a large part in my ugly mood that morning. I fuss and fret for what seems like eternity, before getting to grips with the fact that if I don't leave soon then I'm going to be late for my meeting.

I've decided to take the half-hour walk to the venue in the city centre and redeem myself fitness-wise. It might even make me feel better. So I grab my one biggish bag, laptop and a handbag. Nothing feels too heavy or uncomfortable. Good. I get halfway to my destination before desperately looking around for a black cab. Why is there never one when you need it? All of a sudden my bags feel like they weigh a ton and have become unmanageable. I'm feeling hot, sweaty and annoyed. I struggle on and on with no sign of my four-wheel saviour. My mood is getting darker by the minute.

And then I finally arrive at my destination. I'm ten minutes early – naturally my mood changes again and just like that, I'm feeling good. For some reason, as I press the doorbell, I look down at my bags and up at the sky, and smile to myself. How much worse would it have been if it had started to rain? I did have an umbrella tucked away somewhere, but no hands free to hold it. A strange thought to have at that moment, but it all adds to improve my mood.

What follows is a productive meeting – though earlier I wasn't in the mood to even contemplate the session. In fact, I confess I had even thought about calling and postponing it.

Suddenly my day is getting better by the minute. This time I know I have to walk to the station – but now I am better prepared, at least mentally, for the short haul. I have time to grab a coffee, the paper and even a book before comfortably finding a seat on the train to London. My train arrives on time and my sister is waiting for me at the other end. It turned out not to be such a bad day after all, once I got up and started working towards what I needed to do.

'Those who wish to sing always find a song'

Swedish proverb

Our moods can switch at any moment. Just look at little children. They change moods so naturally, that no one thinks twice about it. They can go from laughter to crying in seconds... and then back to smiling and being happy again all within a minute.

Sometimes we just aren't in the mood to do things. Everything is such an effort or looks like such hard work. I understand that. The key is to do them anyway. Before you know it, the deed will be done and you will be in a different mood altogether.

Your mood actually dictates how well your day is going to go. A woman was going to London for the day and was worried about what would happen. She worried about finding a parking place at the station and fretted about missing her train. She imagined herself getting lost in the big city and not finding a nice place for lunch and so it went on. She felt anxious and what should have been an enjoyable experience was spoilt by her negative thoughts. In the end she had a rubbish day in London. If she had looked forward to the adventure and thought positively about it she would have had a great day.

The next time you think you are having a bad day, take a moment to think about all the good things in your life. Things you take for granted like being able to see everything around you, being healthy, being surrounded by people who care and love you.

What if you didn't have these things? Or all the other great things that make your life easier and better? A morbid thought I know, but it should help you put things into perspective.

Put some music on – it is a powerful way to change your mood. Naturally, if you are feeling a little down, then choose something uplifting to listen to. Go out and get some fresh air – a change of scenery is a good way to change the way you feel.

'I have seen the sea when it is stormy and wild; when it is quiet and serene; when it is dark and moody. And in all its moods, I see myself'

Martin Buxbaum, US editor and author

We all get up on the wrong side of our bed sometimes, but that doesn't mean you should write the whole day off! My black mood had gone through several shades of grey during the day but had definitely ended on the brighter side of the scale. Remember, things can change in an instant – and so can your mood.

'If you can't excel with talent, triumph with effort'

David Weinbaum, US businessman, writer and stand-up comedian

Some people's talent just shines through. They may have to work a little at it, but on the whole, let's face it, what some can do in a heartbeat would take the rest of us months (or years) to achieve. It could be playing an instrument, dancing, drawing, writing, racing, anything at all. When they do it, it is exciting and mesmerising just to watch them and be around them. They make it look effortless, and for a moment, everything else pales into the background.

I experienced something recently that stopped me in my tracks, made me smile and stunned me into silence. Quite a feat, I assure you! I was at a lunchtime Christmas party, and there was the usual chitchat going on around the large room. A number of live acts had been performing on the stage. I heard the music first; a saxophone, the notes so crisp and perfect, the tune so recognisable, the sound so clear, that at first I just sat back in my chair and enjoyed it. Eventually temptation got the better of me, and I turned around to see a young boy on stage, blowing into the saxophone, commanding the stage and controlling the audience. Awesome!

He did a few numbers before rejoining his friend and his father. Quick as a shot, I went over to congratulate him on his superb performance. His father told me he was 12 years old, and had been playing the saxophone for only two years. He went up even higher in my esteem. His father and I exchanged cards. I remember his father saying to me that the family didn't know how to promote their son's talent. I was already thinking ahead to another very big event in the New Year – another opportunity for the boy to dazzle, as he so deserved. I put the boy's family in touch with the event organisers, much to the delight of both parties. As predicted, he was a hit – and so was the event.

I've promised to continue assisting this young boy in any way I can – his talent is one that needs to be exposed. For his part he turns up on time, is professional and delivers an outstanding performance – every time. The audience adore him. It's a win-win situation for performer and audience. If you can help someone along the way, at no cost to you, why wouldn't you?

When you see something that moves you, and you recognise it as a talent that needs to be exposed, do what you can to promote that person – but make sure it is what that person wants. It only works if they agree to the exposure. Even if you mention them to one other person, you never know what it might lead to. Think of someone that you know whose talent shines through. What is it that they do better than anyone else? How do you plan to assist them so that others can see their talent? Who can you introduce them to?

Talent is something that we are born with. It is intrinsic. That means it may not always come to the surface as something obvious and recognised. We may have to search for it and while some people's talent may be quick to spot, for others it may reveal itself slowly over time or may even emerge as a more characteristic trait. For example, I know a lady in her sixties who bakes cakes for the local community centre and her neighbours. She has a real flair for baking and for sharing. She is kind and considerate and never asks for anything in return. Her caring nature is a character trait. It is her talent.

Mozart was a musical prodigy. Michelangelo was a creative genius. Einstein was a master scientist. All were talented and knew what their talent was. I have to work hard at many things, but there are also things that I am good at. I'm aware that they come easily and naturally to me. I know the same is true of you. I don't have one obvious talent that shines through. But that is ok. I'm still searching. . . I know it is in there somewhere.

> *'Of all the things I have done the most vital is coordinating the talents of those who work for us and pointing them towards a certain goal'*
>
> Walt Disney, American motion-picture producer

Everybody has some talent inside them, but most people fail to tap into it or recognise it and so it goes wasted. Sometimes it is easier for other people to see your talent. Listen to what those around you have to say – they may be revealing something about your inner hidden talent.

Combine that with doing things that come easily to you and where you are able to produce outstanding results and you'll be well on your way to discovering your talent. Remember, life is about sharing. Share the talent.

'*Half of the troubles of this life can be traced to saying yes too quickly and not saying no soon enough*'

Josh Billings, pen name of US humorist, poet and writer Henry Wheeler Shaw

> 15 SAY 'NO'

I've heard that the hardest word to say in the English language is 'sorry'. Well, I've found another one. Why is it that some people find it so difficult to say 'no' to others? Maybe you don't want to go out one evening with friends, or spend Christmas with the in-laws, or do the last-minute presentation at work. And just how many times have you come across this one:

'Do I look alright?' Real answer, 'No'.
Delivered answer, 'Yes, fine'.

You get the point, don't you? What is it about that word 'no' that can so easily offend someone? Why do some people say, 'I'll think about it' when what they actually want to say is, 'No, thanks'? We all do it.

I was once asked if I would join a select group of people to help create awareness and raise funds for a prestigious building in Birmingham city centre. The group, made up of influential people, met every two weeks. It was a tempting invitation, and I was extremely attracted to the proposal. However, I instinctively knew I couldn't commit to it; I already had too much on my plate. Yet I really didn't want to disappoint anybody, and I found myself thinking of ways to get around saying no.

First I bought myself some time, saying I really needed to think about the offer in detail. Then I tried pushing it to one side, hoping that it would just disappear under a huge pile of other things I needed to do. Then I even talked myself into considering how I could make it work. I did everything to avoid delivering the true verdict, but I knew in the end I had to give them an answer.

When I delivered the blow, they took it in their stride and were really understanding about my decision. Rejection is never easy to accept, but delivering it in the right way can ease the process for both sides.

I was immediately relieved and impressed at how considerate they had been about my decision. Importantly, it hasn't changed our relationship one iota.

So why did it have to take so long? Where was the benefit in keeping them waiting for an answer and putting myself through the turmoil?

This is what I think happened. I believe everybody has an intrinsic need to feel wanted, desired and loved at the end of the day. I think that when we say no to someone, we believe they will no longer need us, value us or care about us. Ouch, that hurts.

Believe it or not, I've become better at saying no to certain things over the years. I've found that there is no point in doing something you don't want to. I always thought that if I said no, people would think badly of me, distance themselves from me or say unkind things about me.

This hasn't been the case at all. I have found that people appreciate my being straight with them. It means they can put another plan of action in place if they need to. It also stops me feeling forced into doing something I don't want to do, and getting annoyed with myself and others.

'Nothing is so exhausting as indecision, and nothing is so futile'

Bertrand Russell, British philosopher

Being direct, in the nicest way possible, is a great skill to have. Following the 'no' with sound reasoning or a good explanation, both short and simple is often all that is required.

A young woman I know is very friendly and helpful. I was in a car with her and her husband once when a friend of hers rang to see if she could babysit that evening. The woman told her friend that it would be difficult but she would think about it. After the call her husband reminded her that it was just not possible for her to help out on this occasion. She replied she thought she had made that clear. 'No,' said her husband, 'You didn't make that clear, ring her up and just say no'. She phoned her friend again and gave her a clear answer. Dealing with something straight away means everyone can get on with their plans.

The next time someone asks you to do something that you don't want to, try one of these strategies:

Say no straight away and give them a short and simple reason why you can't do it.

Say you will get back to them on it – and use that time to think over the pros and cons of doing what is being asked.

Say yes and get on with what you have committed to – without feeling resentful or unhappy about it.

Make a note of the number of times you say no to something over a week. What did you spend the time doing instead? I promise saying no does get easier with practice.

When I say no it empowers me; I take control of my time and my life. Every time you say no for the right reasons, you make more time to do the things you say yes to.

'I am the awareness that is aware that there is attachment'

Eckhart Tolle, German-Canadian spiritual teacher, motivational speaker and writer

> 16 ATTACHMENTS

We get attached to things really quickly. As a child it's fine to have a favourite cuddly toy or a comfort blanket. Those around us might even encourage it. This childlike need to be attached to things never leaves us.

As we get older, we become fond of different things but we're just more sophisticated in our approach. We continue to be demanding and our expectations grow. We acquire certain ways of doing things and 'need' to have particular things.

Our obsession is not restricted to just inanimate objects: it can be with other people too.

Let's not forget that we can be more in demand as well!

I recently lost my mobile phone (well actually, a pickpocket stole it from my bag while I was sightseeing abroad). I was infuriated, but luckily it didn't change my view of the country I was visiting; after all, the reality is that your phone could be stolen anywhere and at anytime.

What I was really annoyed about was the inconvenience it caused – and, much to my embarrassment, how attached I had become to my mobile!

'Some of us think holding on makes us strong; but sometimes it is letting go'

Herman Hesse, German poet and novelist

The truth is that my mobile is like an extension of my clothes. I feel naked without it. On the rare occasion when I have left it at home, I run to it the minute I get back. If I am going out for the evening, then I'll switch it off, but still keep it close to me. What is the point of that?

I justify it to myself by saying I might need to call a cab at the end of the evening, or have some sort of undefined problem where a phone is a must. It's ridiculous, and I never realised my attachment to it had become so extreme.

Like a bad habit, attachment creeps up on you.

So I'm now back from my short trip abroad and sitting at my desk in the UK; I've been told it will take a few days to get things back to normal on the phone front. It seems strangely quiet. Actually, it feels quite eerie – I'm not sure I like it.

I've become used to the sound of a message arriving or a ring tone. I'm used to rushing to grab the phone, fidgeting with it, checking things on it and anticipating the next call. I also love my speed dial button and the ability to call someone on it – instantly.

And yet, while I have missed it, I have to admit that it is rather nice not to have all those interruptions. I can't recall the last time I experienced such peace and calm. Was this how it used to be before I became attached to my mobile? How quickly we forget that we managed to get things done before our reliance on such technology.

I've continued with my daily business activities, attended meetings and got things done. It doesn't all stop because I haven't got my phone with me; mind you, thank goodness for e-mails.

It can't be healthy to be so reliant on a phone. So I've decided I will make a conscious effort to switch off my phone for at least half an hour every day. How hard can it be? You never really realise how dependent you become on something, until you lose it or stop doing it for a while.

Of course, this doesn't just apply to the mobile, BlackBerry or laptop. It could be something like the clothes you have in your wardrobe. Things that you haven't worn for years or even at all, but just can't let go of.

My friend received a birthday present from her grandparents five years ago. It was a jumper, hat and scarf that she has never worn. She kept it in her wardrobe. She had pushed the items into the darkest corner as far away from the eye as possible. Yet she complained about wardrobe space all the time!

Eventually she had a clearout. She realised that she had been mixing up the affection she had for her grandparents with the need to keep the items they had given her. She had attached the two things together. The moment she understood this, she took them to a charity shop and was surprised to feel relieved and not guilty at giving them away.

We become attached to things for all sorts of reasons. I guess the thing to bear in mind is how loyal we are to the things we get attached to. We may be attached to our mobile, but how long before we want the upgrade? An old item of clothing that sits in the corner of a wardrobe doesn't take the same pride of place that a new item takes. Most of our prized possessions eventually get replaced with new ones. That's just the way it is.

'You can't change the past, but you can ruin the present by worrying about the future'

Author unknown

There is no time like the present. Everything else has either happened, and is in the past, or it hasn't yet occurred, so is in the future. Therefore the current moment is the only real one you have. This may be stating the obvious, but how much time do you actually spend thinking in and valuing the present? It is so much easier to think about things that have already happened or you think are going to happen, and yet the only moment that matters is the one you can control directly. History is important. The past has a place; it has a role to play. We can learn from it and take the lessons it gives us. But ultimately, it stays exactly there – in the past.

Over the years I have looked back over my life on more than one occasion. I've looked at it with purpose and meaning. I've thought about the good times and the bad and I've taken the time to learn what I needed to from the experiences. However I don't dwell in it. I choose to dip into it as and when I need to. So when I've got my public speaking hat on and I'm talking about my journey into the media or business, I need to use examples to bring my story to life – delving into the past proves to be a really valuable resource.

Then there are all those sweet memories – great aren't they? They can make us feel good and bring a smile to our lips. The fact that we revel in the moment of nostalgia makes that memory even sweeter.

There's also the past that mercifully remains exactly there – buried and forgotten. Painful, and only brought to the surface (if ever) because, perhaps, we need to learn something from the experience, or it is stopping us from moving ahead. Good or bad, the past is the past, and you can't change it. But still we say to ourselves 'If only I...', but you didn't – and now it is too late. So focus on what you can do – and get on and do it!

> ### *'In rivers, the water that you touch is the last of what has passed and the first of that which comes; so with present time'*
>
> Leonardo da Vinci, Italian painter, sculptor, architect and engineer

So what of the future? Of course, you can plan for it, prepare for it and wish for it. But the truth is that only the present moment and how you choose to use it can guide and move you towards what you want from life. 'What if. . .' does nothing but stall for time, helping us to create excuses. If you go down that slippery slope, the chances are you won't get much done. You may think of a hundred things and even generate several plans, but you won't have taken the necessary action to move ahead. The reality is that by the time you do, you will have wasted so much time the outcome probably won't be the one you expected. The truth is that nobody can predict what may happen, how someone may react or what outcome you might get.

Many people are scared of presenting in front of others because all they think about is the future. Even before the presentation has happened they're predicting the audience won't like them and they'll be terrible. They build up their anxiety and fear because all their energy is darting towards what bad thing might happen on the big day. What they should be doing is focusing their attention on the presentation itself. If they expended a quarter of that energy towards the material rather than what lies ahead, then they would deliver brilliant presentations.

My friend is in her late thirties. Every time she meets a decent man, she ends up scaring him away. She is so keen to be in a long-term relationship that she actually forgets to take the time to get to know the person first. She is always in such a rush, thinking three steps ahead, she fails to enjoy the current flow that can occur between two people in their first meetings. The actual moment is lost and in its place she plans the future. It is only later she realises that a future with that person doesn't exist.

Tell yourself you will be spending more time in the present and not in the past or the future.

After all, the fact is that right now is the most important moment in your life. The past and future have a place but the only moment that actually counts is the present. Take a moment and ask yourself, 'Am I appreciating the present as I should be?'

'A *project* is complete when it starts working for you, rather than you working for it'

Scott Allen, author

> 18 COMPLETION

Whenever you complete a task and do it well, you experience a feeling of completion. It is a feeling of immense pride, mixed with a sense of peace and fulfilment, all rolled into one. It is the feeling you get after you have tidied up your flat, washed the car, mowed the lawn, redecorated your home or sorted out your filing – at least, doing any of these things does it for me! It comes after you have tackled any task that you have put off for days, letting it grow bigger and uglier by the minute.

Let's take a simple example like putting your clothes away. One evening after work you've been out with friends and return home late. It is only Tuesday and you have an early morning meeting the next day. All you can think about is bed. Leaving your clothes discarded on the floor you jump straight under the warm cosy quilt.

Morning arrives, you're late so you grab another suit from the wardrobe and are out the door in a flash. That evening you arrive home knackered. You cook and after watching a little TV, it is bedtime. You pick up the strewn clothes from the floor and put them behind a chair, to which you add today's bundle.

The next evening you end up working late. You set the timer on your washing machine, so that by the time you get home your clothes have been washed and dried and are ready to be put away. You pick up the whole lot and pile them on the chair. You take one look at the mountain of clothes and exit the room fast. And so it continues.

Eventually the day arrives when you have to tackle the task. First you decide to hang up your suits. That completed quickly, you sort out the clothes, creating little bundles. You pick up each bundle and swiftly place it in the appropriate place. Before you know it, all the clothes have been neatly put away. That completion has actually given you a burst of energy and now you are ready to move on and sort something else out.

> '*The secret of getting ahead is getting started. The secret of getting started is breaking down your complex overwhelming tasks into small manageable tasks, and then starting on the first one*'

Mark Twain, US novelist and humorist

You know as well as I do if you don't start doing something, you'll never complete it and you can apply this feeling of completion to any task. The key is to start doing something, no matter how small. Then you'll be astounded at how much else you will get through – and how quickly! Completion is energising.

Looking at things we don't want to do saps our energy. It makes us feel lethargic and unmotivated when we catch a glimpse of the mountain we have created and so we try to avoid it altogether. For me it has to be tax returns. I have a great accountant, but I still need to pull together all the relevant pieces of paperwork, sift through a huge pile of receipts and sort them under the relevant headings before pulling everything together and sending the neatly bundled package over to his offices. It is a gruesome task to tackle, but amazing on completion.

··· TRY THIS ···

Take a look at a task that you know you have to do but is sapping your energy. It might be something like your filing, or the ironing, or finishing decorating your house. Choose a day and commit to it. Get on and do what you have to do. For example, if it is the filing, then grab all the paperwork. Start sorting it out, under headings like bank, personal, bills, invitations and so on. Once that is done, file them away. Notice what happens to your energy levels.

Completing a task energises us. It makes us feel great, and we enjoy the results so much more. Completion is healthy for us. How long does it last? It doesn't matter. The important thing is to experience it.

*'Have no fear of perfection
– you'll never reach it'*

Salvador Dali, Spanish Catalan Surrealist painter

> 19 EXCELLENCE

My mum always said if you are going to attempt something, do it extremely well or not at all. And she was right. Of course, I didn't quite see it like that as a teenager. I remember doing household chores with my sister when all we could think about was the fastest way to get through the horrible tasks. Any short cut was a good one to take. (Incidentally, the option of not doing it at all didn't exist!)

The truth is that when we do a task and we do it well, it fills us with pride. It elevates us, and makes us feel bigger and better than the best of the rest. Over time, I've stuck with my mother's principle to strive for excellence and every time I put it into practice, I become a better, smarter person.

In a nutshell, striving for excellence means being the best you can be. At the end of the day can you stare into the eyes of the person in the mirror and say you have given it your all?

Excellence tends to be achieved over a period of time. It takes commitment and discipline and the constant need and desire to do better next time. Being the best is something that we have to work at, but you can get there.

When I used to present the news from the studio, there was hardly another soul in sight. The main team were tucked away in the gallery in another part of the building. It is when things go wrong that you learn how good you really have become at the job.

I remember the times when things didn't go to plan, and I had to take control of the situation. So if a report failed to make it in time or there were technical difficulties then I did the best I could to keep the show going, but even a second on air spent like that feels like an hour. I did the painful exercise afterwards of going through and watching how I had done for two reasons. To see how I could improve on my performance, and to put a lid on the incident so that I could mentally prepare and move on for the next bulletin.

When you give something your best then you have achieved a level of excellence for yourself. Do not confuse excellence with perfection. I hear people using that word all the time. They tend to be the same people on a constant mission to have the perfect body, the perfect partner, the perfect home, the perfect everything.

I too used to seek perfection in things until I realised it didn't exist. If something is perfect than it never needs improving, there is no change, no evolving or moving forward. It stays static in its perfection. However, as people we are constantly growing and developing and moving on.

'We are what we repeatedly do. Excellence then, is not an act, but a habit'

Aristotle, Ancient Greek philosopher, scientist and physician

I have met so many people who have dreams of producing the most perfect piece of work. Some have completed the actual work ages ago but continue to hold on to it because they don't think it is perfect.

These same people abuse the word 'yet' to no end. They'll constantly be tweaking or amending their work. They will refrain from showing their work of art to anybody else, afraid it isn't quite perfect. They'll say things like, 'It isn't quite finished yet', 'It's still incomplete'. What they really mean is that they don't think it is good enough. Sadly, even if it is the best they can do, in their eyes it will never measure up to what they think it should be. Put simply it is because they are seeking perfection.

What will eventually happen is that it will never see the light of day. And they'll feel all the worse for it. Seeking perfection plants seeds of uncertainty in your mind. There is no satisfaction to be gained by putting in the hard work to do something, and then see it tucked away, or hidden from sight never to surface.

'People throw away what they could have by insisting on perfection, which they cannot have, and looking for it where they will never find it'

Edith Schaeffer, US Christian author

The point is, this is not about competing with others. Excellence is something you seek within yourself and is about being the best you can be.

What have you been seeking perfection in? Ask someone who you trust to give you an honest opinion about your work. Think about how you are going to raise the bar, and do it better next time.

Competitive excellence is something else entirely. We can't all be brilliant at everything. And no one is asking that of you. You just need to be the best at what you choose to do.

This book is a prime example of what I am saying. If I wanted to make it perfect, you wouldn't be reading it now. I would never have published it. In seeking excellence, I was able to write the chapters, gain the guidance and assistance to shape it, improve it and get it published.

Maybe some of you are thinking this book can't possibly be excellent because there are sentences that start with 'and' or 'but'. However it was more important for me to get my words across to you as if I was actually saying them. So in this instance the excellence lies in the messages that I share with you and not in the grammar.

Excellence is simply about being the best that you yourself can be, in whatever you choose to do.

'The time to relax is when you don't have time for it'

Sydney J Harris, US journalist and author

Time out is compulsory. You don't require anything more than your own company. We are constantly doing things for others, so how about doing something special for yourself? Do you tell yourself, 'I don't have the time...', 'I couldn't possibly...', 'I'd feel so guilty...'? Here's what I say: 'Make the time... you absolutely can – and no, you won't feel guilty!' You don't neglect your family, friends, work colleagues and a million and one other things, so why would you neglect yourself? After all, you are just as important as everyone else on that list and you can't give to the best of your ability if you never take time out for yourself – be a bit selfish from time to time.

Years ago when I worked a television breakfast shift, I had to regularly get up at 4 o'clock in the morning. Every once in a while I would take a snooze in the afternoon. I justified it to others and myself by saying it was because I needed to get up so early. Nowadays, I don't feel the need to justify my time out to anyone. I do it because I want to do it. Time out for me means doing things that I want to do for myself. I don't need permission from anyone, I don't have to impress anybody, I'm self-reliant and I don't even need an obvious result from it.

Sometimes I grab an afternoon show at the cinema – it is a great way to catch up on all the movies I want to see. When my colleagues used to ask what I would be doing with my afternoon, they thought that going to the cinema on my own was a strange thing to do. It didn't bother me. I realised that I couldn't rely on people to be free when it suited me, so I was happy to just get on and do things on my own. Besides, who has a conversation while watching a film in the cinema, anyway?

Other days I might relax on my sofa with a book, the sun's rays pouring through the open windows, a box of chocolates or a tube of Pringles close to hand. Or I might go and look around an art gallery, or go window-shopping. It's great fun trying on things in shops at off-peak times when you don't have to queue for anything, wait for an assistant or battle a crowd. Sometimes I am happy to just sit and listen to some music. Once in a while, I even get my paint pots out and attempt to create that work of art!

The great thing about time out is that it can be anything you want it to be. Sadly, I don't know many people who take the opportunity to indulge in it.

Time out refreshes you, so you can have more energy for others. Failing to take time out is like very slowly starving your body of food or your brain of oxygen. It is like forgetting to put oil in the car. Eventually things will start slowing down and someday you'll find that nothing works as effectively as it should.

I know of a mother with five young children who had a high-powered job. She got her time out every day, because she understood how important it was. For her it was taking the time to have a relaxing bath every night before going to bed. She said it gave her time to gather her thoughts and unwind, so that she would eventually be able to totally switch off and be supercharged for the next day.

Time out helps me recharge my batteries and puts me in a better frame of mind. When I feel nourished and enriched, I am in a position to help nourish and enrich other people's lives. In fact, you don't even have to tell anybody else what you get up to if you don't want to. It can be your own little secret.

Open your diary and block out a one-hour slot. Put 'meeting with me' in the space. Use that time to do something for yourself. What is it going to be? Time out doesn't have to cost anything. But if you really want to spoil yourself then I suggest you book yourself a special treat. You don't always have to wait for a birthday or special occasion to treat yourself. Just go and do whatever it is – you will find that what you get from it will keep you going for at least a couple of months.

So take your time out whether it is once a day, once a week, or once a month. It really doesn't matter. What does matter is that you take the time you need for yourself. Enjoy your time out!

'Sometimes it's important to work for that pot of gold. But other times it's essential to take time off and to make sure that your most important decision in the day simply consists of choosing which colour to slide down on the rainbow'

Douglas Pagels, US author and editor

'True enjoyment comes from activity of the mind and exercise of the body; the two are ever united'

Karl Wilhelm von Humboldt, German philosopher and linguist

> 21 LIFESTYLE

I'm not a teenager any more, and I'm truly pleased about that – apart from when it comes to my fitness regime. After years of trying to keep fit and regularly going to the gym two or three times a week, I thought it would get easier. But it doesn't. In fact, it seems to get harder to keep the fitness level up and the motivation going as I get older. Nowadays if I miss a week or two at the gym, it feels like I am back to square one!

It is my toughest battle; but still I keep going. You see, I refuse to give up on all the things I really enjoy in life – and eating and drinking come high up on that list for me. Looking and feeling good also lies at the heart of the matter.

As a television presenter and public speaker, the image I portray is very important. It takes time to create the person people recognise as Arti Halai; at least 30 minutes of hair and make-up, and understanding what colours and styles suit my personality. It is not something that happened overnight, but something I cultivated over time.

The way I look is part of what makes me who I am. It has taken years to get it right. I was never one to follow fashion trends. At just under 5′1″ and of slim build I struggle to find things to fit me, so my trick is to buy things as and when I get the opportunity.

I'm great at mixing and matching too. I learnt a long time ago it is never about high street stores or designer labels. It is always about how the clothes make you feel. Find a style that you are comfortable with – that doesn't mean it has to be bland and boring or over the top and eccentric. Experiment a little, and eventually you'll create something that works for you.

I believe the way you look says a huge amount about you. Instant decisions are made on that one glance. You know it is true, because you do it too. You only get one chance to make a good first impression. When I look the part it makes me feel good too and boosts my confidence.

'A lifestyle is what you pay for; a life is what pays you'

Thomas Leonard, coach

I'm 39 years old as I write this. When I turned 30 I made a conscious decision that I would start to look after myself better. That meant eating more healthily and doing more exercise. Achieving one out of two isn't bad! That is why I put myself through the weekly gym training.

Don't get me wrong – for me it is always a real struggle to get there. When I go to the gym it is to get the workout over and done with. But what I choose to think about and focus on is how I will feel after the session. I think about how I will look in a beautiful dress, or what I want to see standing before a mirror. . . the latter acts as a particularly strong motivator. Besides you do always feel better after a workout.

Funnily enough, I always thought going to the gym was all about looking the part. Having the right gear: the trainers, the matching attire and the 'look' that goes with super cool, über-fit people. The exercise was just the by-product; getting fit was the ultimate goal, but looking the part was the key ingredient.

I realised very quickly that my thoughts were not based on getting real 'fitness' results. Sometimes it takes someone bold to point out the reality and show you what you need to do to get an achievable outcome. So I learnt the lesson the hard way. There is no such thing as having the right gear to start the training process to get fit. It is an excuse you create to avoid tackling the real task. What really matters is getting the results.

Sometimes in life we have to do things we don't enjoy, but the rewards are far greater. And it doesn't have to be about the gym either. There is no shortage of things to do to stay in shape and keep fit and healthy.

Years ago I read about a Japanese island called Okinawa. The people who live there are the longest-living and healthiest in the world. Not only does it have the highest number of centenarians but it is probably the only place on the planet where you are likely to see 80–90-year-olds living like people 30 years younger. Studies carried out from there show lifestyle plays a key role in their remarkable longevity and vitality.

'Life is not about waiting for the storms to pass... it is about learning how to dance in the rain'

Vivian Green, author

Make sure your trainers and gym kit are the first thing you see in the morning when you get up. Without thinking about anything else, just get into the kit. Keep everything ready, so that you can get going as quickly as possible. Focus on the feeling you will get after your workout. It works better sometimes if you have a friend or partner to share the workout with.

Initially work to a routine but don't make it so rigid that it works against you. For example, it is better to say 'I will exercise three times a week,' rather than tying yourself down to three specific days.

With fashion remember if you have bought something that you haven't worn within the first week or two, ask yourself did you really need the item?

Fitness, food and fashion are all part of our lifestyle. Take the time and care to look after yourself.

'One who asks a question is a fool for five minutes; one who does not ask a question remains a fool forever'

Chinese proverb

Why are people so reluctant to just ask for something they want? I always say that, 'If you don't ask, you don't get!' Not rocket science, is it? I live my life by the rule. I'm happy to admit that if I don't know something, I'll always be the first to ask.

SatNav is great, especially for someone like me who has no sense of direction. However, before it was available, going out on the road as a reporter was a real nightmare for me. I was always getting lost on the way to somewhere or other and the added pressure of a looming deadline didn't help. Pulling the window down or getting out of the car to ask someone for directions proved to be a real lifesaver. Yet, I know some people that will just keep on going in whatever direction, determined they know where they are, when they really don't!

If I want guidance or advice on something to do with my business, I'll call my key contacts and talk through the problem with them. When someone has already achieved what you are trying to do, then chances are they'll have the answers to your questions.

'There are those who look at things the way they are and ask why. I dream of things that never were, and ask why not?'

Robert Francis Kennedy, US attorney general and adviser

Sitting in a restaurant, if I want the chef to tweak a dish that is on the menu, I'll just ask. What is the worse they can say? No? Hardly the end of the world is it? Then again, I might end up with a really special dish, which is exactly what I craved. I'm not even afraid to ask for a hug if and when I need one. Sometimes I'll even ask someone if I can give them a hug – because hugs work both ways!

So why do we find it so difficult to ask for things? Perhaps it is because we might feel silly and small that we don't already know the answer. It may be because we don't want to feel like we are in debt to someone or we owe them a favour. Or maybe it is just because we have never really been taught to ask for help.

··· TRY THIS ···

In the space of a week just ask three people for help about something. It doesn't matter whether you are asking for something or about something. What happened?

Think about the type of questions you ask. How often do you start a question with 'why'? Rephrase that question using 'what' or 'how' instead of the 'why'. What sort of response did you receive?

··· TRY THIS ···

My friend always asks for a discount when going in to buy something at a shop. He takes his time and bonds with the sales assistant first. Then even if the item is on sale he just asks for more money off. Sometimes it will work a treat, and he ends up with a great bargain. At other times the sales assistant will stand firm, but end up giving him something else on top of his purchase. He rarely comes out without a little something extra, and all because he isn't afraid to just ask for it.

I know some property developers. They built an iconic building in Birmingham city centre. When they had their grand vision, the people they were talking to kept saying 'This can't be done'. When they asked 'Why not?' nobody really had an answer. So they went on and built it anyway. Today it stands as a shining example about what can be achieved when you just ask the right sort of questions.

That's another thing. Take a moment to think about not only the question you are asking but also how you are asking the question.

You may have heard the saying, ask a better question and get a better answer. I'm careful when I ask a question using the word 'why'. Often, unintentionally, it can lead us up the excuse or blame route. I prefer to use 'what' or 'how' at the start of a sentence instead. I find it gets both me and others thinking more proactively.

Then there are those times when you might not even get an answer to your question. Still you'll never be worse off for asking it. After all nobody has the answers to everything. That is just life. Still, with nothing to lose and everything to gain, your job is to get on and just ask.

"'I must do something"
always solves more
problems than "Something
must be done"'

Unknown author

> 23 RESPONSIBILITY

Responsibility can weigh heavy on our shoulders, can't it?

It can make us feel important, too. Probably the most powerful lesson I have learnt to date is to take responsibility for things. Don't shy away from things when they go wrong or, even worse, point the finger and blame someone else.

At times we can be really fast with that one!

When things go wrong, as they sometimes do, the first thing that people in businesses and organisations do is look to pass the buck. The focus quickly moves from what happened to who is at fault. The blame game kicks in.

I have no problems with getting to the bottom of things. The steep learning curve often serves us well. We learn quickest when things go wrong. I have no issue if somebody or a group come forward and admit they made a mistake. But the truth is, that doesn't happen often.

I was presenting a news bulletin early one morning. The director was very young, and new to the role. He accidentally pressed the wrong button, and instead of the bulletin going out on air that morning, a static graphic with the message 'normal service will resume soon' went out.

I spoke to him afterwards, and at first he said it was a fault with the technical equipment, and then he said his instructions from someone else hadn't been clear.

Eventually he admitted it had been his mistake. He had accidentally pressed the wrong key. Once he took responsibility for what had happened he changed his thought process from feeling powerless and afraid to taking action. He clarified what had happened, admitted the mistake was human error and forwarded suggestions about how to avoid the problem in the future.

When you take responsibility for a situation, it empowers you, and as a result you are far more likely to take some form of action. You can move forward much more quickly when you accept that you had a role to play, no matter how little, in something that went wrong.

Failure to do this will leave you feeling trapped and frustrated for days to come, if not longer.

Always acknowledge your part in a failure or when things don't go to plan. Once you get your head around this concept, you'll become far more comfortable with yourself, achieve so much more and improve your relationships with others.

'A chief is a man who assumes responsibility. He says "I was beaten", he does not say "My men were beaten"'

Antoine de Saint-Exupery, French pilot and author

A few weeks ago I was training a group of people. I had prepared some workbooks for the course, which the organisation had agreed to print and bind for me. On the day of the course I felt happy and excited, and arrived early to set up the room as I wanted it.

I saw the workbooks from the corner of my eye. To my horror, they weren't printed as I had expected them to be. They looked like poor quality work. My mood quickly changed. I was angry and annoyed. I realised I would have to use them, but made a mental note to find out who had messed this up.

Before the group arrived, I made a conscious decision to focus on the material I was going to deliver. I took the time to get back into the 'zone' and the training went really well. Incidentally nobody even seemed to notice what the workbooks actually looked like, though a few people did comment on how useful the material inside them was.

Sometimes when things don't turn out exactly like we expected them to we lose perspective, and look at just the worst-case scenario. I understand now that I was being overly critical about the workbooks, and actually they didn't look as bad as I had thought. However, I still needed to find out what had gone wrong.

I took a moment to assess the situation properly. What became clear to me after a while was that I had not been specific enough with my instructions. I had assumed the organisation would know what I wanted. When I saw the situation in that light, I realised I was just as much at fault, if not more, for the poor quality of the workbooks.

Whatever the circumstances, we all have a part to play in the world of responsibility. So next time the tide turns and things don't go according to plan, you know what to do.

'You must take personal responsibility. You cannot change the circumstances, the seasons, or the wind, but you can change yourself. That is something you have charge of'

Jim Rohn, US author and entrepreneur

'The simplest things are often the truest'

Richard Bach, US author

'Life is so complex'. I hear that all the time – but it doesn't have to be that way. I like to keep things simple. I find it is the best way to learn, understand and appreciate things properly.

I first became aware of this when I started speaking in public; an event that once terrified me, but that I now wholeheartedly embrace and teach to others. Over the years I have seen so many presentations where the audience has switched off and yet the presenter keeps droning on and on. More often than not, there is just too much complex information crammed into the tiny slot allocated for the talk. The best presentations are where the speaker keeps things simple and never loses sight of the key message. Very few get it right.

So why do we feel the need to make things far more complex than they have to be? You know it's true. Perhaps it's our fear of looking stupid or not being convincing enough, our lack of confidence in ourselves or our need to look important and in control. Whatever it is, try to peel back all the layers and really get to the heart of the matter. That sort of clarity will help you make a much better decision. Always see the situation for what it really is.

'Life is really simple, but we insist on making it complicated'

Confucius, Chinese philosopher

I went on an interesting personal development course last month. At the time I couldn't get my head around the point they were trying to make. It was a three-day course – and by the end of the first day, I felt I had got very little from it. Everything had been 'woolly' and rather vague. I couldn't get to grips with the key message they were trying to put across.

My friend, who had previously been on the same course, told me to persevere with it. He assured me it would all click into place, but I have to admit I wasn't entirely convinced. Still, I stayed with it and completed it. It was an unusual experience.

Now the penny has dropped. It was this concept of simplicity in our everyday tangled lives that they were trying to get us all to understand. What lies at the crux of an issue really boils down to a few very basic things. All you have to do is separate the facts from how you choose to look at a situation. Definitely easier said than done! Admittedly, most of us are better at doing this when we are looking at someone else's situation.

We lead cluttered lives. Our situation is often clouded by all sorts of other things; but making a decision about anything really comes down to one of two things. Yes or no. It really is as simple as that. Simplicity gives us a better understanding about ourselves and others. It forces us to slow down and see a situation for what it really is.

'I finally figured out the only reason to be alive is to enjoy it'

Rita Mae Brown, American writer

Simplicity isn't found only within us humans. It can also be found in nature. Sometimes appreciating the simplicity in our surroundings and our environment helps us too. Take a walk in the park or the countryside and enjoy the moment. Actually notice the beauty of nature; the sound of the birds; the wind. Take a walk along a beach; look at the sea, your surroundings, the sky. It moves us and yet there is nothing complex there. Neither should there be.

Sometimes when I need to remind myself about simplicity, I go to the florist and buy a single rose, taking a moment to appreciate its beauty; the intensity of its colour, the folds of the petals, its texture, its shape. It reminds me that things don't have to be complex. Nature isn't complex. Life doesn't have to be either. Keep it simple.

'It's not the work that's hard, it's the discipline'

Author unknown

Discipline – I'm not so good at this one. I know I will have nailed it when I can condition myself to get up at the same time every morning, without using an alarm clock. Some feat!

The fact of the matter is that we all need some degree of discipline in our life. The cynics among us may cry that discipline keeps us tied to a regime and a certain way of doing things. The truth is it makes us more productive and efficient – and without it we wouldn't get very much done.

I'm a list person. I tend to make lists of things I need to do, and then tick them off as appropriate. I can make the list anywhere I want to, adding and subtracting things as I go along. It keeps me on track, and it keeps me focused on what I need to do and what my priorities are. It is an example of a discipline that I have created in my life. If only it were always this easy.

Going to the gym at seven o'clock in the morning for a workout would be a good example of being really disciplined. Would I do it if I didn't have a personal trainer, waiting to put me through my paces? No, I know I wouldn't.

Here's the test. Do I go to the gym at that time of the morning on any other day of the week? No. So I am only disciplined when I have to be – but that isn't necessarily a bad thing because I'm achieving what I set out to do. Discipline doesn't need to be regimented and inflexible. I find looking at discipline in this way works much better for me. Whoever said discipline was one-dimensional?

Running my own business means working to my own timetable – and that certainly requires discipline. If I am working on a particular project then I'll set myself certain targets to hit by certain times. I become more disciplined and focused then, and it tends to be more productive for me to operate in that way. Discipline can lead to good practice and good behaviour.

'Success is nothing more than a few simple disciplines practiced every day'

Jim Rohn, US author and entrepreneur

Every book I have read about a successful person says the same thing. These high achievers are where they are because they lead disciplined lives. Take a look at any sports personality, the armed forces, the Shaolin monks or other martial arts masters. Discipline lies at the centre of their universe.

'Discipline is the soul of an army. It makes small numbers formidable, procures success to the weak, and esteem to all'

George Washington, army commander and first president of the United States

The son of a friend of mine had a spending problem. He didn't think twice about buying something he wanted. Basically he was spending more than he was earning. A substantial debt soon mounted and he defaulted on payments. The bank put his interest rate up to stratospheric heights. That's what banks do.

My friend stepped in and decided to help by paying off half of the debt. He asked his son to pay the money back with a low rate of interest on a monthly basis. This worked until his son missed a payment. My friend went ballistic and they had a full and frank discussion about the way ahead. The penny dropped and his son suddenly got the hard reality of the situation. He changed his ways and put stringent financial rules in place. He became extremely disciplined about the way he used his money and came to realise that if he could not afford it he had to do without. It took him five years but by the end of that time with those disciplines in place he finally paid off his debts.

There is a lot to be said for discipline. It is to be admired and respected. Without discipline you get disorder and chaos; with it you can create purpose and substance. When all is said and done, the truth is that very little is actually achieved without discipline. So embrace it and make it work for you!

'*Think more about who you are and less about what you do, for if you are just, your ways will be just*'

Meister Eckhart, German theologian and philosopher

Just be yourself.

Well, are you? What is it like to just be yourself? A lot of the time we are playing a role, whether we realise it or not. It doesn't matter where we are, whether it is at work, at home or at social events; we take on certain ways to behave, act and react, depending on who we are with.

So what is wrong with that? Nothing. But you do need to be clear about the different roles you play in life – and there are plenty of them. Together they help shape the person that you are.

I used to say I was a television presenter when people asked me what I did. It was easy. I never even thought of it as a role I played, it was just me. Then when I lost my job, it got me thinking about who I really was.

Somebody kindly pointed out to me that I had lost my identity. I had tied in *who I was* with *the role I was playing* in being a television presenter. It was how other people saw me, and it made it easier to define me in those terms.

Put simply, your identity and your role are two different things. Your role is what you do. Your identity is about your character and personality. This is what makes you who you are. Your role is something that others can see and recognise. It is external. Your identity is built within you. It will come out through your behaviour but it is something that is moulded internally.

I met a really bright graduate who was working in a big law firm. He was clearly doing well and establishing a name for himself, not just within the company but also in Birmingham. He told me that when he first met me, he didn't even know I worked in the media. He just knew me as Arti, and it was 'me' the person, that he had bought into.

> ## 'Unlike a drop of water which loses its identity when it joins the ocean, man does not lose his being in the society in which he lives'
>
> BR Ambedkar, Indian philosopher

Sometimes it is difficult to separate who we are from what we do because we live in a society where we like to define people by the roles they play; it is easy and allows us to put the person into previously defined pigeon holes.

I was the guest speaker at a woman's networking event one day. I met a woman who had come along with her friend. When I asked her what she did, she looked embarrassed and said, 'Oh I'm just a housewife'. That is not the first time I have heard that statement said in a shy, resigned voice. These are women who create and look after their homes, the children, the family and do numerous other things. Why do they find it so difficult to say proudly and confidently, 'I am a housewife'?

Think about what the role entails. Just because it doesn't pay in the conventional manner, it doesn't mean it isn't contributing something of real value. When you understand how much value you actually bring to something, then you start to see yourself in a different light.

We have certain perceptions and expectations when someone tells us what they do, whether they are a dustman, a teacher or an entrepreneur. Most of it is tied in with money and status. That is why it is so important to understand more about your identity rather than the roles you play. The ability to value yourself will make you feel proud and confident, and it is that inner feeling that should stay with you, no matter what it is that you do in life.

'Nobody can make you feel inferior without your consent'

Eleanor Roosevelt

How many different roles are you playing in life? What are they? Write them down. Take just one of these roles. What does this role involve? Be specific. How much value are you adding by what you do? What characteristics do you need or have you acquired while doing this role? Take another role and ask the same questions. Can you see the difference between the roles you are playing and how the value you bring is tied to your identity? This is not about money, status or background. It is about valuing yourself and what you have within you.

... TRY THIS ...

When you can be yourself, regardless of who you are talking to, then you are at your most authentic.

'Make the most of yourself, for that is all there is of you'

Ralph Waldo Emerson, American author

Reminding yourself what you have learnt from the roles you play and how you plan to use those lessons will assist you in moving forward much faster than if you choose to hold on tightly to a particular role.

The other great thing about coming to grips with the idea that we play lots of roles is that if you lose one, you still have several others to hold on to. So, for example, if you've lost your job, then that affects one specific role you have been playing. It doesn't make you a bad father, brother, friend or mentor. It really is about keeping things in context. It won't be long before you find a replacement role. I know – it happened to me.

'There are some people who live in a dream world, and there are some who face reality; and then there are those who turn one into the other'

Douglas H. Everett, author

> 27 THE REALITY

Sometimes we delude ourselves because it is so much easier to enjoy a rosy picture rather than reality. The grass always looks greener on the other side doesn't it? We look in awe at the glamorous lifestyle of a movie star; the success of an entrepreneur; the recognition bestowed on an eminent scientist and we want it.

What we lose sight of are the hours of hard work, discipline and steely determination that go into getting that end result. We just see the glossy cover – it is the surface of the shell that excites us. The reality, when we open our eyes, is always somewhat different.

I remember years ago I was working at a radio station when I got a surprise phone call from a cousin of mine. The job was my first foray into the media industry. The hundreds of hours of work experience had paid off, and I had landed the job, through sheer commitment and hard work. I hadn't seen my cousin for quite a while. Our paths rarely crossed and we weren't particularly close. So when she called me one day out of the blue and asked to come and see me, I was intrigued.

She arrived one evening and as we sat drinking tea, she told me she wanted to follow in my footsteps and chase her dream to work in the media. She was starry-eyed and in awe of what I did because back in the early 1990s it was still rather novel for an Asian girl to work as a broadcaster in the UK.

I asked her what she had done to get a foot in the door. I was curious to hear about her experiences in local community radio, hospital radio or university radio. She told me she hadn't done any of those things. Not deterred, I thought maybe she had tried her hand at the local newspaper, as I had done at the age of 16. No, she hadn't done that either.

It became clear that she was looking for a quick ticket into the world of broadcasting. She wanted contacts and introductions into the industry. I told her the reality of the situation. I explained what my role involved. The hours I worked, the two-hour, one-way daily commute I endured to get to the radio station, the work experience placements I had done, the commitment I had shown to set me on the right path. She listened.

I told her I was happy to assist her if she could prove to me that she was serious about working in the media. But I wouldn't make the necessary introductions until she was ready. The reasons I gave her were simple. First, it would be unfair to the company I worked for and second, I didn't think she would survive very long with that laid-back attitude.

What I gave her was a reality check. I told her to contact me again at a later stage. She never did. It hasn't spoilt our relationship. I don't even think badly of her. I just think she needed someone to tell her like it really was. She had bought into the grander illusion. All I did was put her back in touch with the reality.

'Few people have the imagination for reality'

Johann Wolfgang von Goethe, German writer and polymath

TRY THIS ...

What would your dream job be? What makes it so attractive? Now find someone who is already doing that job, or something similar. Get them to tell you what the work really involves. Do you still want to pursue the dream? If you are sincere then the reality behind the job should never put you off.

TRY THIS ...

I know some people who have dreamed of a better life. They have uprooted and moved the whole family to another country. Within a year they have come back to the UK because the life they had imagined abroad wasn't the reality they experienced.

Have you ever met a film star? If you have, then you'll agree a lot of times they seem much smaller in real life than how you imagined them to be. The wider picture sometimes looks better than the close up.

The truth is, we need both the reality and the dream in our everyday life. The reality helps keep us grounded but we still need to fire up the imagination, create the dream and indulge in the illusion. We spend far more of our time doing the latter rather than the former and that is no bad thing. After all – it is all about living the dream.

'*Everyone is a millionaire where promises are concerned*'

Ovid, Roman poet

> 28 PROMISES

If you say you are going to do something, do it. Or don't make the promise. It really annoys me when someone says, 'I'll call you back in ten minutes...' and then doesn't. I understand something may have turned up or a meeting may have over-run, but that doesn't change the fact that the call didn't come, and I waited for it. It immediately leaves me feeling disappointed.

A much better approach would be, 'Can I call you back later in the day, next week...?' Then the expectation isn't there. I'm just as guilty as the next person on this one. I've promised to call at certain times and then for whatever reason failed to do so. When one of my sisters pointed it out to me, I stopped doing it.

Awareness is a great thing. Nowadays, it is very rare that I will give a specific time to call anyone, unless it is a conference call (where due to the number of people involved you obviously have to give an exact time).

Of course there are exceptions to the rule – aren't there always?

My thoughts on promises are like my thoughts about business or about your health – really simple. In business, make more and spend less. With health, eat less and exercise more. With a promise, if you commit you need to deliver.

Yesterday I called a client. He told me he was busy and asked if he could call back at a particular time. I agreed. I sat at my desk, with my laptop open and true to his word he called at the suggested time. Within five minutes we had sorted out what we needed to talk about because we both knew the nature of the call and were totally focused on what we had to do. It was a pleasant and efficient phone call. Naturally the conversation started well because he kept his promise to call at a certain time. It put us both in the right frame of mind. For your part, if someone says they are going to call you at a specific time, and you agree to it, then you have to make sure you are free to take their call.

If you promise to call someone at a specific time then make a note of it in large writing and place the note where you will see it.

If you fail to make the call, for whatever reason, then make sure you get them to point it out to you next time.

It will make you aware of what you are saying and you will avoid making the same mistake again.

Sometimes we promise to do something because we feel under pressure, or maybe we just want to get away quickly or we feel the need to look good in front of others. The reason doesn't matter. What matters is that if you have agreed to do something you have to see it through to the end.

If you agree to deliver something by a certain date, work hard on keeping that promise. In some cases it will be impossible to hit the deadline; things out of your control can happen. Then tell the person that you are doing everything you can to meet the target, but you may not be able to. It might be that you both agree on another outcome altogether. That is much better than letting the person realise that you have not delivered on time and waiting for them to get in touch with you. You made the decision. The choice was yours.

'Promise only what you can deliver. Then deliver more than you promise'

Author unknown

Actually if you are going to promise to do something, then you may as well go the extra mile; people will always remember it.

The thing about telling someone you will do something is that you create an expectation – and they then rely on you to deliver. I've seen promises just roll off some people's tongues:

'I promise I'll be there on time'
'I promise I won't forget to. . .'
'I promise I'll do it'

I'm not saying for a moment they wouldn't have made good their word. I'm merely saying we're quick to make promises.

Politicians are notorious for promising the earth, especially in the run up to a general election. Very few actually come good on their promises once they are in power. As leader of the former Soviet Union, Nikita Khrushchev said, 'They promise to build bridges even where there are no rivers'.

Traditionally, a promise was an unbroken bond, like a gentleman's handshake. It was a serious commitment that came with serious consequences if undelivered. It was important and it went hand in hand with trusting someone. I met a couple who recently celebrated their 60th wedding anniversary. My own grandparents have been together for a similar period of time. They promised to stay together till death do them part. Of course, this situation only works if you promised to make each other happy too!

So you can call it whatever you want to – a promise, a bond, a deal, a commitment – just as long as you are clear about what it means to both you and the person you have agreed it with. Don't lose sight of what you stand to lose should you fail to deliver on your word.

Be careful about the promises you make. Times may have changed, but some things really do stay the same. A promise is a promise.

'Be firm on principle but flexible on method'

Zig Ziglar, US author, salesperson and motivational speaker

29 UNDER PRESSURE

If something isn't working for you, stop doing it and try a different approach. Simple, isn't it? Only we don't always see it like that. Sometimes we get so caught up in events that we can't see the wood for the trees. Trying to force a square peg into a round hole is never going to be a good fit. But at times, we can be so close to the problem that we can't see where we are going wrong.

Unknowingly we keep doing the same kind of thing. We fool ourselves into thinking that if we tweak something here or there, everything will come right. We get absorbed in the problem, turn the pressure up and let it go round and around in our heads. It is only when we take a clean break from the situation, step back and see it with fresh eyes that we can gain clarity on things and assess the situation properly.

A few years ago my friend brought some properties to rent out. He redecorated them and then went to a well-known DIY store to choose some furniture. I agreed to help him assemble the kit when it arrived. We unpacked the flat packs and checked all the parts were intact. With toolbox close to hand, we set to work assembling the relevant bits and pieces. Luckily my friend proved to be a dab hand at reading the instructions. We were coming to the end of building a rather complex wardrobe, when we both stopped in our tracks. We realised we had too many pieces left over, and that we had missed something out. We couldn't spot the obvious mistake. We went over it again and again. Eventually, exhausted and late into the night, we decided to complete the job in the morning. On arrival the next day, we both spotted the mistake straight away.

Sometimes things get distorted because we choose to look at them through a magnifying glass when all we really need to do is take a step back. We were both so fixed on looking at the situation in one way and the pressure to find the problem was so intense that it clouded our judgement.

When you start to let go of built up pressure and learn to relax a little you will see things in a different light. It's like when you are trying hard to remember the name of an actor in a movie, or the singer of a particular song. It doesn't matter how much you rack your brains, you just can't remember it. Then when you least expect it and you've given up thinking about it, bang it comes straight into the forefront of your mind.

TRY THIS ...

Have you got a problem that you just can't see a solution for? Leave it alone and return to it in a few days time. You will find you are in a better position to assess it. Keep an open mind and make a list of all the options you have. When you are open and willing to be flexible in your approach, the answer will present itself to you.

... TRY THIS ...

When you release the pressure and take a breather, you relax instead of being tense and closed about the situation. Being adaptable and flexible in your approach are also components in oiling the wheels for the way forward.

Personally, I'm a stickler for things – so if I make plans I like to stick to them. However, I understand that things don't always go according to my plan. Sometimes meetings get cancelled at the last minute, or somebody says they'll do something and then fails to keep their promise. If you acknowledge that these things might happen, then you'll stop being really disappointed when something goes wrong.

You have to be flexible and open in your approach. That means always remembering that things can change, because quite frequently they do. Remaining rigid only puts you under unnecessary pressure. Being flexible is all about dealing with situations as and when they happen. It is about trying a different approach to get things going again.

'The only pressure I'm under is the pressure I've put on myself'

Mark Messier, Canadian hockey player

So let's take that cancelled meeting. Being flexible means you can focus that time and energy on something else that needs doing instead. At the end of the day it is never about what goes wrong. It is always about how you deal with things that go wrong. The key to that is to take a step back, release the pressure and do something else in its place. You are more likely to get things right when you do not feel under pressure.

'The road of life twists and turns and no two directions are ever the same. Yet our lessons come from the journey, not the destination'

Dom Williams Jr, US novelist and poet

No journey is like a straight line. It takes all sorts of twists and turns to get to your final destination. But of course, you have to know where you are going, so that eventually you can get there!

Today, however, I'm not looking at the end result: I'm taking a moment to reflect. I'm interested in thinking about the journey. The moments that you experience when you get sidetracked; the things that build your character and make you the person you are.

I've taken several wrong turns in my life. Some were harsh lessons to learn, others pleasant surprises. Regardless of which they turned out to be, all of them have made me a stronger person, and I'm glad for the experience.

When I first started in the media, I applied for a bursary that was available for a technical assistant. The truth was that I had very little interest or experience in the technical aspects of radio. Even at the time, I must have known deep down that it wasn't for me. But I was desperate to get a foot in the industry door and that is all I thought about. I honestly convinced myself that getting a place on the scheme was my only chance.

I struggled with the tests that were a part of the interview process. When I was told I didn't get the place, it felt like my world had fallen apart. I cried and cried. What was I really crying for? My tears had not been at my failure to secure the technical assistant post. They had been for what I saw as a missed opportunity.

The reality was that I really wanted an editorial post, but for a moment I had become blinded by the fog of an opportunity. I had become desperate in my quest and had tried to grab anything and everything. That rarely works.

Eventually another opportunity surfaced, and after months of work experience and proving my commitment, I got the job. The rest, as they say, is history! So for a while my route had become cloudy; still I never lost sight of the destination.

While waiting to secure my first job in radio, I had to supplement my work experience with a job that brought in an income. I ended up working in a ladies' fashion department store. Now I look back at it I know it taught me about customer service, style, and it also gave me some insights into business. I don't see it as a wrong turn. I look at it as taking the scenic route. Sure, you may have even lost a little time, but what new things did you experience as a result? There have been lots of other little detours like that along the way.

Unfortunately, the truth is that we rarely take a moment to stop and look back at the journey we have taken so far. The first time I thought properly about it was when I had to address some students about my career in the media. I decided to weave my story using examples and the big lessons I had learnt on the way over the years. I realised my experiences and achievements showed clearly that I had a lot of self-belief and determination. It also highlighted a characteristic that I had never considered myself to be – ambitious. I never realised what a powerful exercise it would be.

Take a moment to look back at all the things you have achieved. Reflect on the mistakes and pitfalls, the lucky breaks and the successes. Think about how you continued on your journey regardless of everything, and how it has shaped you. Share your story with someone. It will help you realise what you have achieved and it will also reveal your strengths.

TRY THIS ...

Looking back at your life doesn't just have to be about your career. Perhaps you've lost a lot of weight and have changed your lifestyle over the years or maybe you are taking the time to reflect on all the people who have helped shape your life to date.

'We may run, walk, stumble, drive, or fly, but let us never lose sight of the reason for the journey, or miss a chance to see a rainbow on the way'

Author unknown

I read something in a book that really made me think. The author asked the reader to write what they thought people would say about them after they died. A morbid thought I know, but also an extremely effective one.

How do you want to be remembered? What is it that you want people to say about you? Ultimately we all want to feel cared for, needed and loved. We want to be treated with respect and admiration.

For me there is no single magic formula. It is more a combination of lots of different things. Trial and error is just as important as getting it right first time. In the end when you are able to feel good about yourself, then you are able to make others feel good about themselves.

I'm coming to the end of my book now – writing my final words to you. It has taken me six months to write this book. I was full of fear and trepidation... remember that monster? I confronted it head on – and I'm really glad I did. In some ways writing this book has been a cathartic trip. Frustrating, challenging, exciting and insightful, but I've learnt new things about myself along the way and it has been an interesting experience.

The truth about the journey of life is that we take lots of turns along the way, but the actual destination remains a very long way off. It is rarely about our final destination, anyway. It is the journey that counts; the interesting and revealing route it takes as it unfolds and leads us to new adventures.

In these pages I've shared with you some of my journey and what makes me who I am. Your journey is an integral part of who you are. It is your adventure. Your life. Consider your journey. When you do, you will realise what a very long way you have come.